*Scenes from
Spanish Life
c.1930*

Scenes from Spanish Life
c.1930

ANN LIVERMORE

With a Memoir by
HAROLD LIVERMORE

UNICORN PRESS
LONDON

Unicorn Press
76 Great Suffolk Street
London SE1 0BL

email: unicorn@tradford.demon.co.uk

First published 2002 by Unicorn Press

ISBN 0 906290 68 6

Typesetting by Ferdinand Pageworks, Surrey
Printed in Great Britain

Contents

Foreword

Ann's residence on earth filled most of the twentieth century, in the middle of which she set down these reminiscences of Spain; she refers to them variously as tales or scenes. There were two more, both relating to Andalusia. One was a visit to Falla: they have disappeared and must be considered lost. Her first love was for music, and particularly for the music of Spain, on which she wrote. She was not a regular concert-goer or -giver, but enjoyed singing for its own sake and in less formal guise, whether teaching school-children in Portugal or overhearing the Brazilian poet Cecilia Meireles in the adjoining hotel bedroom. She also liked thinking and writing, having acquired from her mother a sound grounding in Shakespeare. Her excellent ear helped her to write dialogue: playwriting was no mystery for her. Her reading was varied and constant: after Shakespeare came Shelley, Stendhal, Shaw: she constantly scribbled notes. She passed easily into the study of art, particularly after acquiring Sandycombe Lodge, still haunted by the spirit of J.M.W. Turner.

It is not easy for me to write about Ann. I ought to mention those whose lives contributed to hers, but to name only some of those who are still living would be invidious. Of those who are no longer resident, I can think of Charles Aubrun (Hilda is happily still with us, though well into her second century), Eric Blom, Casals, Ivo Cruz, Luis Díez del Corral, Hilda Finberg, Concha Gallostra, Patricio Gannon, Santiago Kastner, Michael Kitson, Denis Millman, Joaquín and Victoria Rodrigo. I should mention the support of her brother and sisters.

I should thank Mrs Fernanda Roberts and Andrea White for their indispensable help in preparing this book, and also the friendly Unicorn.

H.V.L.

Ann (Mason) Livermore:
A Memoir

PART ONE

ANN WAS THE SECOND CHILD OF Thomas Edmondson Mason and
Margaret Lapraik and was born in Hampstead on October 8 1903.
Her father came from Howden in Yorkshire and was born in 1841. He
was a grazier and the principal butcher in Hampstead. His first wife
Catherine died in 1899, without children. He then married Margaret,
who came from Waterside by the Doon in Ayrshire, and loved litera-
ture and music and had given recitals of Shakespeare. She gave Thomas
a son and four daughters, of whom Ann was the eldest. The family
lived at the shop in Hampstead High Street, and the nursery was above
the stables. It had a piano. It was apparently a very happy childhood.
'Nancy' was a serious child, whose talents were soon recognized. In old
age she loved to exchange nursery anecdotes with her sister Margaret,
who survived her by less than a month. The girls outnumbered John,
though they greatly respected him. He attended University College
School and studied law. As a solicitor, he was always helpful and never
litigious. Nancy went to South Hampstead High School. She remem-
bered hearing Elgar play his cello as she passed on the way to school.
She played the piano for assembly, and greatly admired her English
mistress from whom she acquired her love of the language and its lit-
erature. Her sister Dorothy was more practical, and was said to be the
first girl in Hampstead to own a motor-cycle. The family were
Methodists and welcomed their kin from Cumberland and Scotland
who came to London for the 'May meetings.' Ann was independent
enough to leave one chapel for another because the music was better.
She studied the piano at the London Academy in Kensington, which
gave her its gold medal in 1925. Her father died in 1927, and as he
aged her mother struggled to keep the business going. Her brother was
not yet established, and Ann earned her first money, a pittance, by
playing the piano in the silent cinema. At a students' concert, the

Hampstead and Highgate Times noted 'no less enjoyable was the play-
ing of Ann Mason, a clever pupil of Miss M. B. Hoskyn': her interpre-
tation of Bach was pleasing, and her touch 'delicate and clear.' By 1929
she was writing as music critic for the same paper. When the pianist
Solomon gave a concert for the benefit of his old school King Alfred's,
she noted his generosity and his excellent technique, but hinted that his
treatment of Scarlatti was a trifle heavy. She had no doubts about her
own taste, and could adopt a slightly magisterial tone for a girl in her
mid-twenties: 'one is glad to record the success of an amateur orches-
tra', which had on its side time for rehearsal and enthusiasm, she
thought this one able to tackle a more ambitious programme: 'I should
imagine them capable of bigger things.'

Her interest in Spanish music was aroused by the discovery in a
Hampstead bookshop of a copy of J.F. Riaño's *Notes on Early
Spanish Music* (Quaritch, 1887). It included several autograph letters,
and cost five shillings, which she persuaded her father to give her.
However, her knowledge of music was general, and I know nothing
of how she took up singing or came to specialize in Spanish music. I
suspect that she found English taste (if such a thing exists) conven-
tional: I say this because she called her essays on literature 'exploring
literary territories.' In 1930 she was in Spain and had the experiences
recorded in these *Scenes*. They are not stories, but impressions
adorned with what her brother called 'Nancescan embroidery.' In
1930 – the year before Spain exchanged the monarchy for the disas-
trous Second Republic – she studied singing at the Madrid
Conservatoire with Ignacio Tabuyo, known as 'Toby.' She recalled his
dignified reception as he opened the door with 'Adelante, señorita!'
She had studied Bach, Handel and Mozart in England with Carrie
Tubb, and in Paris French music with the Brazilian-born Vera
Janacopulos, who sang Falla's *El retablo* in London in June 1927. At
that time Paris was still the centre of international innovation in let-
ters and music, and she moved on the periphery of its activity. Her
ability to travel was probably assured by her marriage to a young
English banker, whom she taught to play the guitar. She did not say
how this happened, or how it broke down. Some cuttings show that
she was in Barcelona in June 1931, when she heard a new group
called Compositors Independents de Catalunya. In an article pub-
lished in the *Daily Telegraph*, she noted that Falla was himself half
Catalan: the eight members of the new group included Toldrá,

Mompou and Robert Gerhard, the last the enfant terrible of the move-
ment. He had returned from Vienna, where he had been a pupil of
Schönberg. He had gone the whole way in the matter of atonality but
Ann looked forward to hearing his versions of Catalan popular songs:
he had the positive virtue of finishing when he had no more to say.

In April 1932 Ann contributed to the *Daily Telegraph* an article on
English music in Spain. She recalled that Arbós and his Madrid
Sinfónica had played Elgar as early as 1905, but that it was Saco del
Valle's Orquesta Clásica, founded in 1929, that had a great success
with Holst. The private knowledge of English music in Spain was
marked by a woeful if understandable ignorance: one conductor of a
choir boasted that he knew the two best English songs, which were
'God save the King' and "Home Sweet Home'. This she found fairly
typical. When she returned to London, she settled in the Hampstead
Garden Suburb and in February 1933 drew up a brochure as a
teacher of singing. In a letter to the *Radio Times* she took issue with
J.B. Trend, 'so distinguished and delightful a writer,' about
Mompou's supposed indebtedness to Les Six and on a slip in speak-
ing of Granados. In another letter, she commended the BBC for a pro-
gramme of two guitars, but suggested using the bandurria: for
listeners outside Spain, this was an acquired taste, but that was all the
more a reason to cultivate its acquaintance. Her article on Granados
in *Music and Letters* (June 1933) drew an appreciative notice in the
Hendon etc. Gazette, which identified here with music in 'the
Suburb'. She was beginning to make a name for herself as a music
critic, and the article on Granados combined delicacy and insight
with a literary charm often lacking in musical critics. These qualities
she undoubtedly possessed. they were wedded to an urge to proclaim
the truth as she saw it: of a Spanish concert on the BBC, she wrote in
the *Radio Times*: 'English voices were entirely unfitted for the music,
having none of the sharp, bright incisiveness of Spanish women.' The
English tended to be pleasing where the Spanish were poignant. One
is inclined to think that the English expect passion of Spaniards, yet
do not much care to hear it. Ann herself joined with the English con-
sort of viols in a programme of old Spanish music given at the Casa
d'arte in St. John's Wood under the patronage of the Belgian and
Spanish ambassadors (the novelist Pérez de Ayala) and Dr Albert
Einstein. The local critic regarded this as a 'song triumph': Ann sang
with 'quiet reticence which became the music and words.'

In May 1933 she contributed an article on Spanish and English music to the *Monthly Musical Record*. She noted how unknown Spanish music was in England, even the Golden Age of Encina, Guerror, Cabezón and Fuenllana, and the two greatest of all, Morales and Victoria. If Handel, born in 1685, was to cast a long shadow over English music, Domenico Scarlatti, born in the same year, was as dominant and lasting in Spain, to such as extent that the 'brave tunefulness' of the English idiom and the 'daring and variety of the Spanish' seemed wholly submerged. The flood of Teutonic romanticism indeed nearly drowned the surviving local traditions. But, as in England the native voice was heard in light comic opera, so too it was in the Spanish Zarzuela. 'Their chief composers – Bretón and Chapí – are as well beloved as our Sullivan, and their works are as popular as the Savoy operettas.' She instanced performances in some little town in Spain where in a programme of almost Oriental length, three works have been rushed through before a mixed matinée and evening audience, which appeared as simple and as beamingly delighted as any 'Savoyards.' She thought that, 'with the shrinking of the Teutonic gods in the present century, the time had perhaps come for a new creed of nationalism in art, perhaps in protest against the growing internationalism of daily life.' England and Spain were on musically parallel lines; they should learn to know one another better. Falla and Turina were familiar, but not the younger generation, first Ernesto Halffter, then Gustavo Pittaluga, and in Catalonia Robert Gerhard and Baltasar Samper. In Spain, English music, Purcell, Elgar, Bax, Holst, were listened to 'without that prejudice which in France, Germany and Italy, caused by our alleged 'unmusicality,' often seems to prevent people from hearing it with open ears.'[†] Ann's reference to Scarlatti seems to have been taken up by Edward Dent in writing his commemorative article in October 1935.

On November 26 1933 Barcelona saw a Nicolau Festival and on December 2 a Homage to Falla. Ann wrote of both in an article on 'Music in Barcelona' in the *Monthly Musical Record* (January 1934). Of the Orfeo Catalá, she observed that it was doubtful if the 'dry almost vinegary tone of the trebles and sopranos would generally please a northern ear', but she was struck by the likeness of the

† On the death of Elgar in 1934, it was Falla who was selected to fill the vacancy for a foreigner in the Institut de France, proposed by Paul Dukas.

Orfeo's tone to the popular cobla.' Evidently much of the applause was political. The Falla festival in the Liceu presented a brilliant, though not a gay scene, which was hardly surprising in view of the gathering national tension. The standard of the artists in 'La Vida Breve' was neither musically nor historically worthy of Falla's opera. With few exceptions, theatrical conditions in Spain were still chained to the realism of stock companies of the last century. The dancers in 'El Amor Brujo' were effective, but the grouping was conceived in a school of naturalism unfamiliar to English audiences. The orchestra was the backbone of the performance.

Falla himself directed his 'Nights in the Gardens of Spain'. During the rehearsals he completely changed the orchestra's conception of the work. The pianist was Frank Marshall, who had been taught by Granados. He told Ann: 'I have played often enough with him but now I find his whole interpretation altered. This is a performance for the few, not for the general public, which prefers the music taken much faster, always seeking a feverish alliance brilliance in the style of English and American musicians. The whole work is transformed into an evocation of the spirit of ancient Iberia.' This great change in his attitude towards his own music seemed also to apply to all his vocal works. At a private gathering the following Monday night, Falla and the Conchita Badia d'Agustí – 'one of the world's finest singers today' – went through his vocal works. 'There was no less intensity than of old, but the lessening of the nervous urgency and the pushing on of the tempi revealed a changed outlook and a further stage in the development of Falla's art. Does this presage some profound development in the *Atlántida* which has absorbed him for so long?'

In 1935 she studied in Barcelona with Conchita Badia d'Agosti, the most accomplished Spanish singer after the premature death of the extraordinary Conchita Supervía, in London and in childbed, on March 30 1936. Supervía had become a great opera-singer, but Ann went primarily in search of the music of the Spanish people, as she says in these *Scenes*. Through Conchita Badía, Ann was invited to visit Casals at Vendrell. Spain was already moving under a shadow.

Ann returned and gave a recital of her Spanish songs at the Mercury Theatre in November 1935. The programme began with two of her favourites, 'El jilguerito,' by Blas de Laserna (1779) and Ernesto Halffter's setting of the poem by Alberti 'La corza blanca'. She sang songs from Felipe Pedrell's great collection, Granados,

Roberto Gerhard and Toldrá, ending with Andalusian songs. For all these she had provided translations into English. Carrie Tubb had sent her an encouraging letter: 'I hope you are feeling in the pink and ready for the fray. Don't do too much and keep the bloom on your voice.' Apparently she did. The critic of the *Morning Post* wrote. 'It was a pleasure to hear such an assured rendering of the Spanish songs. Her interpretation was vital and sensitive. Apart from her technical command, her songs were ardent and convincing.'

The reverse page gave details of Mussolini's war in Ethiopia.

A Memoir

PART TWO

THE SPANISH CIVIL WAR IS now all but forgotten by most Spaniards. Outside of Spain it continues to be fought in the minds of politicians and historians who still turn over the carrion of propaganda. There is nothing new about civil strife or even about the use of force to attain political ends, but it was first advocated as the only way of obliging the rich to disgorge their possessions by anarchists and by communists, following the teachings of the intellectual incendiary Karl Marx. It was furthered by the lurking ambition of Americans to cast the world in their own image. The civil war in Spain was touched off by the French politician Léon Blum, who thought that he was clever enough to manage the communists by forming a 'Popular Front.' If France sneezes, Spain cries 'Jesús!' There were anarchists in Spain, but hardly any communist party until the Socialist Youth was taken over. I had witnessed a similar attempt in Cambridge, though its consequences were less dire. I graduated in 1935, and on the recommendation of the first professor of Spanish, J.B. Trend, was awarded the Hispano-British Society's Award to study in Madrid: it alternated between Oxford and Cambridge and this was Cambridge's turn. My father had been an invalid, and my mother in her widowhood had made I know not what sacrifices to keep me going. I was glad of the award, which was to be held at the old Residencia de Estudiantes. I think I was supposed to study liberalism in Spain, but in fact devoted my time to reading what I had not read at Cambridge. The formation of the Spanish Popular Front outgunned the generation of intellectuals who had implanted the Republic in 1931. Among my fellow-students, I saw young socialists adorn their rooms, barely furnished in the sober style of Giner de los Rios, with pin-up portraits of Comrade Molotov. The electoral campaign of 1936 was conducted largely as a personal attack on politicians accused of corruption. Azaña, the father of the Republic, addressed mass meetings on a scale hitherto unknown, and won a substantial victory in the elections of February 1936. He was promptly hoisted into the presidency, where he had little influence. The atmosphere remained tense. I went to Seville for Holy Week. There were rumours that the government might forbid the traditional religious processions. It did not. I made my first brief visit to Portugal, taking the night train from Salamanca to Oporto and stopping everywhere. An elderly Frenchman had told me: 'C'est là-bas que les trains vont doucement.' From Oporto I went to Santiago de Compostela, where the streets were plastered with demands for a 'statute' of autonomy, but the atmosphere was calm. I returned to Madrid by train, and as we crossed the Guadarramas in the light of dawn, wearily, we heard the newspaper boy crying the assassination of Calvo Sotelo, at Ávila perhaps. By July 1936, it was no longer possible to work. The libraries were shut, and at night we were kept on the hop by indiscriminate shots from *pacos*. General Mola, who launched the insurrection, was soon killed in an air-crash. The Montaña barracks, not far from us, rebelled, but was quickly reduced when cannon were brought up. In the Residencia, the students who had all been on familiar terms divided into knots: the fabric of society was coming apart. Many left for their homes. The British Embassy urged families to take shelter in its garden. It was soon crowded with tents. I took a look and decided it was not for me. At length, I agreed to be evacuated and took the night-train to Valencia, the only sea-port accessible from Madrid. A British destroyer was waiting in the port to carry the evacuees to Barcelona. We travelled on deck, ate sardines, and watched the flying-fish in the sunlight. We slept on a cruiser in the harbour of Barcelona, and next day were carried by another destroyer to Marseille, and so by train to England.

The Republicans negotiated with the Basques, offering them autonomy, and the Basques, led by the footballer Aguirre, accepted. Their Navarrese cousins gave their full support to the insurrection, now commanded by General Franco, who turned his forces on the city of Bilbao. It was reputedly defended by an 'Iron Belt'. Much bloodshed was expected, and it was decided to evacuate several thousand children to England. It was now the summer of 1937, and they were brought to a field at Eastleigh near Southampton, and lodged in army tents until they could be distributed to centres to be organized throughout the country. They were accompanied by teachers, auxiliaries and priests. There were urgent appeals for help, and among those who responded was Ann Mason. She became an expert at combing and washing heads for lice, at attending to all sorts of needs, at accompanying groups to their destinations. The ignorance of do-gooders and others passed all understanding. The children were divided into catholics and non-catholics. In England, non-catholics were automatically protestants, and juvenile Marxists, who had been taught to abhor religion, were therefore protestants and consigned to the Salvation Army. The discovery that there were 'protestants' who knew no hymns and had not been taught the Lord's Prayer caused no little astonishment. The much-heralded Iron Ring proved to be only a Maginot Line. It became clear that Bilbao would fall in a few days. There were confabulations about how to break the news to the children. The priest were for imparting the news after Mass. Some psychologists said that the children be adverted on the loudspeaker system and informed *tout court*. The psychologists had their way. The children were bidden to pay attention and told that Bilbao had fallen. There arose a kind of howl or scream such as I had not heard before and do not wish to hear again. Then someone cried 'A Bilbao!' and almost the whole crown bolted for the gate, which was rushed. Some teachers tried to stem the tide, but in vain. The smaller children soon fell by the wayside and were rounded up. Others had gone for miles. Night fell, and search-parties still combed the surrounding roads and lanes.

By September, the weather was no longer suitable for children to live in tents in the open. Distribution was much slower than had been foreseen. Those remaining at Eastleigh must be moved elsewhere. The new site was in huts at Dymchurch in Kent, close to the sea and by the road and sea-wall. We resumed our task. Ann still washed heads, interpreted, sang and accompanied. I do not remember what I did. Perhaps I checked lists. I was supposed to teach some English: there was a blackboard, but I did not know how to teach. Ann's birthday, October 8, came and went, with presents from her mother. I forget completely when she and I left, separately, but in touch. She probably lasted longer than I did. I returned to the Reading Room of the British Museum and to Cambridge.

A Memoir

PART THREE

MUSIC BROUGHT US TOGETHER AGAIN. Professor Trend was devoted to the Second Republic, and helped stranded intellectuals as best he could. Conchita Badía came to England, and was to give concerts. She brought here accompanist Villalba and his wife and the composer Roberto Gerhard and his wife Poldi. Ann put some of them up at her flat in Hampstead. Conchita was to give a concert in Cambridge. None of the party knew English. Trend asked me to accompany them by train, explaining why they should go third-class. I picked them up at Ann's. She did not accompany us. Trend had arranged a concert at the Town Hall. There was some announcements in the streets. But nobody in Cambridge knew who Conchita was, and nobody came. Or very few. Spain was a battleground so foreshortened by the journalists that nobody was supposed to have time for music, unless for propaganda. It was rather like the story of the old Irish lady who organizes a ball with orchestra and forgets to send out the invitations. One who came was Camille Prior, the energetic wife of the Professor of French, who did her best to explain and soothe. I hope I learned something about the importance of attending to detail.

When Ann and I married, I still had no visible means of support. I had informed my mother, who had ambitions for me, but was careful not to say precisely when. It was a quiet affair, attended mainly by Ann's sisters. She wore a green tailored suit. It had too many buttons, and I told her so when tact ought to have prevailed, but she was sufficiently in love not to mind. I remember that the registrar examined the documents with attention and warned me that if they were not correct the marriage might be Vullanoid, I think an original Spoonerism. They were, and it lasted until Ann's death in 1995. Our means were very limited. We lived in rooms not far from Ann's old school in Hampstead. Her piano and other possessions were put in store. We both went daily to the British Museum, where I read Spanish history. It happened to include Portuguese, and I wrote a novel about King Sebastian's catastrophic African campaign in 1578: I did not think it worth publishing, but submitted it to one publisher, who apparently thought the same. We talked a good deal about literature, and devised a story for a comedy. She read William Archer's *Playmaking* and showed a, to me, amazing facility for writing dialogue: she had finished the comedy before I had time to work it out. The reading about Isabella II (which also remained unpublished) provided her with material for a play using scenes from the Spanish nineteenth century: she called the play 'Pity she's a Queen.'

From this unpromising situation we were extricated by Cambridge University and by Trend. I recall that Trend had introduced me to C.P. Snow, an ambitious scientist fascinated by the machinations of politicians, about which he composed several well-written novels, which sufficed to make him famous. Snow soon detected in our talk that I had no political ambition and was therefore of no interest to him. I felt sorry for Trend. But the University had the Gibson Award, which was for economics or Spanish. I had not read economics and the Spaniards were still in the throes of war and ineligible for serious study. The rules were gently bent to enable us to go to Portugal. One of my fellow-students at Madrid, Leonard Downes, who had graduated from Glasgow, had just been appointed to Coimbra University. The British Council had begun to operate in Portugal, making George West its representative, and naming Downes as director of the Casa de Inglaterra in Coimbra.

Soon after our marriage I had taken Ann to meet my mother, who was staying with her sister in Herne Hill. Ann was dressed in sober black. The encounter was awkward, but not chilly. My mother had nourished hopes of a splendid career for me, imagining a first-class at Cambridge to be a sort of passport. So it was, if you had means, but not for the only son of an impoverished widow. Good relations were soon established, and it was from my mother and aunt's house at Cliftonville that my uncle drove Ann and me to Tilbury to board the *Highland Brigade*. Our resource would suffice for a stay of a few months. It was springtime, and as the ship sailed by the Kentish coast the apple-orchards were in blossom. We rounded the Foreland and ploughed through the Bay of Biscay to Vigo, where emigrants came aboard and the diet altered, and so to Lisbon. We landed and proceeded to Coimbra, where we lunched at the Café Nicola, the most elegant in the city: we had steak with an egg on top followed by strawberries and cream and coffee, which cost all of twelve and a half escudos. Downes and his wife Doris found us a *pensão*, that of Doña Adélia dos Santos, Rua Alexandre Herculano 17. It was frequented by visitors; a judge from the north and his wife coming for medical treatment, the old Visconde Sobral and his wife, the mathematics master of the *liceu*, an English theologian, a doctor, two well-to-do students, who sat at a separate table. The maid of all-work was Teresa, who accompanied her mistress to market, made the beds, washed the floors (always last thing on Saturday nights) and practically everything else: she looked probably twice her age. The cook was Casimira. I went daily to the splendid baroque library of King John V, where I had a carrel overlooking the river. Ann went to the music-school where she practised. She met Arminda Correia, a talented soprano and teacher, who gave her Almeida's Spinalba and the works of João de Sousa Carvalho, the Portuguese Mozart, the arias from who opera O *Amor industrioso* Ann introduced in London. She also acquired Portuguese popular songs, including the collections of Francisco Lacerda and Luis de Freitas Branco.

Conversation with our table-mates helped me to wring some of the Spanish out of my Portuguese. It was varied enough. The mathematics master had emigrated to New York without knowing any English: his first job was on the underground, calling 'Watch your step, Watch your step.' Later he became press-agent for a boxed, Santos Camarão, the Portuguese Promo Carnera, an enormous fellow who was soon laid out and retired to keep a tavern at Ovar. The Visconde believed football inelegant, and was all for courtesy and fencing: his wife used to slip subsidies to their nephew, who opened a cinema to show religious films with the approval of the bishop: there were not enough religious films to keep it going and he soon had recourse to less elevated fare. The English theologian was observed sweeping the forecourt of a church. Somebody reported this to the consul in Oporto, thinking our friend to be slightly touched. The consul came down and interviewed the supposed lunatic in the room next to ours. The prospective lunatic explained that he was distressed to find the church neglected. The consul retired.

Our stay was lengthened by my catching a fever which brought my face out in black spots. Doña Adélia absolutely refused that I should go to the University Hospital, where her husband had died. He had been a minister and she was convinced he had been done away with by foul play. Ann and Doña Adélia dabbed my face every few hours. Casimira made me *canja*. Ann went to the kitchen to tell her it was exquisite. Casimira buried her face in her apron and burst into tears. *Esquisito* is queer or odd.

The Downes went on leave, and I was engaged to look after his library. The outbreak of war drew daily nearer. One of our fellow-guests was the American Arabist, A.R. Nykl, who held that war was a necessary form of population-control: war was God's Flit. It was not a view acceptable to the Portuguese.

Ann liked to stroll in the cool of the evening to the Botanical Garden where the doves cooed as they came down to drink at the fountain. We would meet old Mr Behr and his dog and talk about the world's affairs and our own. Mr Behr had been a typewriter repre-sentative in Lisbon and could remember the Revolution of 1910 and the anarchist bombs of the early twenties. When he retired, he had gone to London, stood in Piccadilly Circus and considered. He knew nobody in the metropolis and nobody cared about him. He returned to Coimbra, his dog and an open car he had. Before the war, the Ministry of Information gave him a job, renting a shop in the window of which he displayed a model lion and a miscellany of leaflets.

We were due to return to England by ship. As we travelled by bus to Lisbon, war was declared. Our ship did not arrive, having been ordered to put into the nearest port, wherever that was. The agent had no news. We stayed in a pensão, reduced to one meal a day, for which we could not pay. I sent a telegram home, but either it was refused or no reply was permitted. I went to George West and asked if the British Council had any work for me. it had as soon as term began. We then moved to the rectory of the British church, a spacious building of the later eighteenth century, in which British merchants were confined during the brief Napoleonic occupation. The rector, Reverend Fulford Williams, and his wife Violet used to let the upper floor to nurses from the adjoining British Hospital. Fulford Williams, a Devonian, had been chaplain to a dozen regiments in the Indian army, and was much visited by passing officers and seamen. Fulford's black retriever Grouse had the run of it, but was prone to escape, on which occasions he was arrested by the stray dog unit. The Portuguese were well aware of the danger of stray dogs, and Grouse had to be rescued from the city pound before he was disposed of. He returned wearing a sheepish expression.

Ann sang in the church, and was in demand as a soloist at weddings, which Fulford conducted in his own peculiar way. On one occasion Ann sang at the wedding of two parishioners, neither in the first bloom of youth. Fulford began is allocution by informing the happy couple that marriage was not a question of dealing a good hand and playing it well, but ... The antithesis remained unspoken.

It happened that the headmaster of the English school at Carcavelos went to England for an operation and did not return. I was duly appointed his successor. I had acquired some teaching experience, but was ignorant about school subjects and had no knowledge of accountancy. Carcavelos was on the line from Lisbon to Estoril, and the building, the Quinta Nova, had been given by Pombal to one of his collaborators. It had been used by Cable and Wireless as their training-station and equipped with a gymnasium, a cricket-ground and two villas: the sea was at the bottom of the estate. It had been relinquished as a training-station during the great slump, and had been converted into a school. With the war, English families preferred not to send their children back to school in England. There was also a Portuguese section, and numerous refugees from Europe enlivened the atmosphere. We were asked to take in a score of Poles, who knew only their own language; we put them in a separate class until they had enough English or Portuguese to be incorporated, which was not long: their vocabulary was small and they were young and anxious to learn. Religion presented no problem. The priests, Anglican (Fulford), Catholic, Scotch, gave their services first thing on Monday mornings. Our single Jew sat by himself. By ten o'clock the clergy were free to teach Latin, causing some problems, since each had is own idea of pronunciation. Our Catholic, formerly of the Propoganda Fidei in Rome, treated Latin like Italian, our Oxford graduate had the restored English pronunciation, Fulford unrestored Cambridge as used in 1910, and our Presbyterian made it a dialect of Scotch. We acquired a piano from an old English lady in Sintra, and Ann delighted in teaching singing. The children performed *A Midsummer Night's Dream*, and she taught them the songs. I doubt if she was ever happier. We had a flat, the piano, our food, servants, and a hundred pounds at the end of the term.

Ann resumed her singing career. At the Academia de Amadores da

Música, she sang songs by Morley, Ford and Purcell in a concert organized by Jorge Croner to Vasconcelos, an outstanding pianist and teacher whose memory was recognized by an exhibition at the Belas Artes in 1999. She sang 'with perfect style' – 'obteve carinhoso acolhimento revelando escola e linda voz.' She found a capable accompanist in Dennis Brass, then with the British Council. He gave a talk on Purcell, as background for Purcell's arias. The programme was given in Lisbon in January 1942, and repeated at Coimbra and Oporto. In Coimbra, the freshness of her voice earned her the phrase 'juvenil cantora de magníficos recursos vocais, elegante apresentação e uma bela voz, bom estilo e boa escola.' In Oporto, she sang the best pieces of the famous composer – Purcell – with a crystalline voice to great applause: the manner in which it was presented was as interesting as it was novel. In June 1942 she was back in Coimbra to give a concern of Handel, Mozart, modern English composers and 'those Spanish songs which Ann Livermore interprets so well,' and a week later the *Anglo-Portuguese News* referred to a 'notable evening of British music such as Lisbon has not heard before,' The *Seculo* said that all the works received brilliant interpretations and won prolonged applause from a large audience, and the composer Rui Coelho, writing in the *Diário de Notícias*, called her a soloist with a great knowledge of ancient and modern music and a 'voz muito simpática.'

Ann was glad to be praised in the eloquent language of Camões. She would probably have said that the composer to whom she owed most was Henry Purcell. Dido's lament from *Dido and Aeneas* was always warmly received: 'we heard for the first time Dido's lament from the English soprano who sang with musicality and great dignity.' The same programme included Vaughan Williams, Britten's 'Seascape,' Delius, Bax and the Somerset folk-song 'The water is wide.'

A Memoir

PART FOUR

ANN'S MUSICAL JOURNEYS IN PORTUGAL were not without their difficulties. Transport was problematic. There was little petrol: some cars were adapted to gas and pulled the necessary equipment on a trailer. The rail line from Lisbon to Cascais was electrified and reliable. But there was no coal, and long-distance trains burned wood, which had to be replenished from cords placed on the station platforms. The burning wood gave off sparks that came through the open windows and made burn-marks on the upholstered seats. There were frequent stops and long waits while the tenders were replenished. When Ann went to Oporto, some two hundred miles, I used to ring to find out how the train was getting on: on one occasion she arrived seventeen hours late. There was always sufficient food, even if mainly fish, rice and potatoes. A retired Dutchman had cows and paid his little daughter's school-fees in pasteurized milk, which we sold to other children: she came to school on a donkey with the milk-cans dangling on either side. When Hitler had his famous interview with General Franco on the Pyrenean frontier, there were fears that the Generalissimo might give way, and that we might be invaded. I was instructed to have sacks of rice prepared and to map a path to the beach in case of evacuation. General Franco proved a good deal better at handling Hitler than Neville Chamberlain had been. That fear was soon banished.

My constant harassment was in finding staff and getting pupils through English examinations with or without the required textbooks. One or two masters had gone back to England and the number of pupils had increased. I acquired some books when the English school in Oporto closed. But for teachers, I had to stop refugees coming through from Europe. There were very good schools in Europe, some were excellent, but the pressure from refugees was such that we could rarely get work-permits for more than a year. There were long queues outside the police-station at which papers were examined and requests granted or refused. From time to time I received circulars urging me to return to England to assist the war-effort. Would I not be better employed in England'? I was fit enough, except that my appendix was oddly placed and rumbled on occasion: I had no time for an operation, but used to keep an x-ray handy in case a surgeon needed to know where to find it. Eventually, I succumbed. The British Council was able to get young men of military age admittedly some very eccentric – but the school governors seemed unable to help, though the Shell representative was invaluable in doing the accounts. I decided to quit. I suppose I was young and arrogant. I had satisfied my mother by becoming a headmaster, not a bishop. Ann; as usual, accepted my decision. We sold the piano and other possessions, and left our papers with friends. We had arrived in Portugal with a couple of suitcases for a short stay in the spring of 1939: we returned similarly in November 1942, but of course we carried memories of Portugal with us.

We set off from Sintra, then the airport for Lisbon. Neither Ann nor I had flown before. It was a November day with a clear blue sky. The regular service between Lisbon and London was maintained by the Dutch. It was commonly believed that the planes were not interfered with, because both sides obtained information through Lisbon, which was a hive of gossip, if not intrigue. I had a seat by the window. Ann sat beside me in a state of extreme tension. The steward brought us lunch, some sandwiches on a tray. The plane was fairly full. There were children playing in the aisle. Ann asked the steward when we would put down at Oporto. She intended to get off. The steward replied that they did not now put down at Oporto, but flew straight out over the sea: it was safer. Ann said nothing, but sat stiffly by me. Suddenly there was a loud cracking sound and the windows were shattered. The pilot made a dive towards a patch of cloud that had appeared on the sea's surface far below. We were soon covered by a veil of mist. The fighter did not pursue us. The plane straightened, and the distance from the surface of the sea seemed to level off. I held my plastic tray over the window to stop the rush of air. The spray of bullets fired from below had gone through the windows and into the roof. Nobody was hit. Ann became quite relaxed. I asked her how she felt. She replied with a smile: 'Glad I've always been good.'

A Memoir

PART FIVE

WE CAME DOWN SOMEWHERE IN Devonshire. When we got out, we saw that the nose of the plane was riddled with small holes. We thanked the captain and pilot, who had to go back and do it again, on one occasion with fatal results. We were transported to Bristol, and telephoned Ann's family from the hotel. Next day we took the train to London, and joined Ann's mother, brother and sisters at Finchley. My mother had given up our house in Lincoln and moved into a small cottage, with no telephone. She had crammed in all the furniture in case we might want it. I reported to somebody or other, and was interviewed. I seemed unfit for the ranks. Nobody seemed to know what to do with me. I was asked if I would join the overseas service of the BBC. I replied that I would rather not do propaganda for anyone. I told Professor Robin Humphreys, who had been leaving Lincoln school as I entered it. His father was headmaster of the school in which my uncle George taught. He had read history at Cambridge and taken up Latin American history. He had now entered Arnold Toynbee's Foreign Office Research Department at Oxford. I went to Oxford, saw Toynbee and Sir Alfred Zimmern, and was appointed to the Spanish and Portuguese section under Professor W.C. Atkinson of Glasgow. We went to Oxford, and lived in a hotel until we found a lodging-house. The department was at Balliol College, and my office in a Victorian tower where we examined newspapers and other material which might have useful information. Anything likely was marked with red pencil and cut and pasted up by female graduates. Ann sang in a concert for the Prisoners of War Fund. She gave her Spanish and Portuguese songs, and found an excellent accompanist in Dr, later Sir, Ernst Chain, the co-discoverer of penicillin with Fleming, and recipient of a Nobel Prize in 1946.

I met Professor W.J. Entwistle, the eminent professor of Spanish at

Oxford. He knew that I had completed my History of Portugal, which I gave to the University Press in Cambridge, then run, almost entirely I think, by S.C. Roberts and his trustworthy pencil. Mine was a lengthy book, and paper was rationed, so progress was slow.

Meanwhile, somebody in authority had decided to merge us with an economics department and move us to London. I saw my mother in her overcrowded cottage in Lincoln. Soon after, she suffered a stroke, and I saw her for the last time in hospital. I do not remember if she recognized me. She died soon after, and as I was deluded enough to think my work important, Ann went to the funeral instead of me. My mother used to say that she did not care if she was buried in an orange-box provided that people were kind to her on earth. She was sixty-two, and had worn herself out looking after my father, who had died just before I went to Cambridge.

Ann and I moved to London. We were given a day to make the journey. Salter's river-steamer still plied between Oxford and Kingston, with a night at Reading, and stopping at British Restaurants for meals. We travelled as far as Reading, where we got off to complete the journey by train. There were no porters, and Ann stood by the bags while I fetched a trolley from the station. We returned to the Mason house in Finchley. Dorothy had married a Canadian soldier. Jack was a fireman. Barbara was a land-girl in Shropshire. Margaret looked after their mother. Jack's connections found us a flat in Hampstead, on top of the highest block, and not the most beautiful of buildings. It had no lift, but was large and roomy: getting Ann's piano up the stairs was a quite a job. The Foreign Office had set aside quarters for the department in St James's Square, next to Toynbee's Chatham House. It was furnished with trestle-tables and chairs of deal. I remember little of it, for we were not there very long. The security people examined it and wanted to build a wall on the roof to prevent unauthorized access. The Fire Service would not permit this for fear we might not be able to get out. We had missed the blitz, but the flying-bomb was still to come. We were accordingly obliged to move again, this time to the Old Stationery Office, built in the nineteenth century for members of Parliament to keep their carriages. The floors were connected by ramps. It was said to be the only building in London designed to keep horses upstairs. Painted dark green and cream, it was just the thing for temporary civil servants.

Ann resumed contact with the Vukotič family, whose children had been at Carcavelos. He was a Yugoslav diplomat, and Mme Vukotič was an excellent pianist and a pupil of Respighi, whose songs Ann took up, especially 'Settembro'. Mme Vukotič also introduced her to Cunelli, an Italian teacher of *bel canto* in London. With her usual thoroughness she devoted herself to the exercises, and by the spring of 1944 she was ready to give a formal concert in London. Singers are their own instruments and are vulnerable to inflammation of the tonsils or quinzy, which obliged her to postpone the occasion. It finally took place on May 5 at the Wigmore Hall. The critic of the *Times* wrote: 'Miss Ann Livermore's song recital at the Wigmore Hall last Friday was devoted to music from Spain and Portugal, and the programme was as interesting and unusual as it was colourful. At first it seemed that Miss Livermore had made a mistake: what we heard might well have been Mozart, and yet on the printed programme there was the name of Sousa Carvalho, an eighteenth-century Portuguese composer from whose opera *Amor industrioso* this aria was taken. It was an interesting example of the internationalism of music of that period when even the rhythm and accentuation of language caused no outstanding departure from the main stream of European music. In the Portuguese popular songs and the Falla's ' Seven Popular Songs' the national flavour was strong. The two groups were in striking contrast, not so much for geographical reasons as for the interpretation of the word 'popular' in each case. The Portuguese songs were simple in emotion and in their strophic structure and thrummed guitar-like accompaniments, whereas in the Spanish songs it was only the sentiments of the words which could be called 'of the people.' Falla's highly cultured settings make considerable demands, not only on the understanding, but also on the voice and on the pianist. If rhythmic vitality is the outstanding feature of Spanish music, then the songs by Granados were more romantic than national in feeling. The aria 'La maja y el ruiseñor' from the opera *Govescas* must surely be one of his most poignant and beautiful utterances. Miss Livermore, who is an English singer, had obviously made a considerable study of this music and was wholly in sympathy with it. She had great variety of expression, even if not always that little extra touch of vividness commonly a associated with the Spanish temperament. She was heard to best advantage when singing softly. An aria such as that by Granados needs big soaring tone, and at times Miss Livermore was apt to harden. Mr Ivor Newton played the exacting accompaniments with brilliance.'

On coming out, someone said, I suppose for me to hear, that they were reminded of the great Supervia. For Ann, the performance was something of an ordeal: she remarked that she would rather not have to go through all that again. She probably thought of teaching. She had a few pupils, but had little patience with mediocrity and none at all with vulgarity of any kind.

She liked small and less formal occasions. One of her problems was with accompanists. The brilliant Ivor Newton was adept in all styles, but he was greatly in demand and could earn high fees. She could perfectly well accompany herself, but she liked to introduce each song and could hardly do this from the piano. She conveyed what she needed to Ian Stirling, who often played for her in London and sometimes further afield.

Trend offered me a junior lectureship at Cambridge. I accepted. It was poorly paid, and I continued to do a day or two a week at the Old Stationery Office. Toynbee had been succeeded by a Cambridge historian, E.J. Passant, who was kindly helpful. I used to go to Cambridge by train, and spend a night or two at the house of Mrs Scherchen, who had been the wife of the well-known Austrian conductor and then lived in Cambridge. The train service was terrible. The compartments were unheated. I used to catch the evening train after the day's teaching, and the delays were reminiscent of Portugal during the war. Sometimes it was almost midnight before I got to Hampstead. I was then told that I ought to be resident in Cambridge. I found a house in Chesterton Road overlooking the river and the extensive grounds of Jesus College. There was room for Ann's piano, and we could let the upper floor and garret. Ann sang at the Music Club, but I do not have the programme. Trend was kind to me. Ann may not have been too accommodating: he was a musical journalist and a prolific writer, but she was the professional musician and critic, who published articles on Granados in Geoffrey Sharp's *Music Review* (May 1946) and Eric Blom's *Music and Letters*. A letter from Eric Blom, then editor of the latter, of April 1947 thanks Ann for three studies on Portuguese opera and offers her some publications of the Instituto Interamericano de Musicologia; if she wants it, 'I will send it with pleasure – chiefly, I admit, the pleasure of getting it out of the house!' In more tactful vein, he adds 'I was much amused by your contrasting Oxford and Cambridge so much in the former's favour ... I do confess to a penchant for Cambridge, as a town at any rate. I'm sure the goings on are much the same at both places, but seem worse at the one you happen to be living in. I expect if you lived at Oxford, you would find a visit to Cambridge just as refreshing.'

I had more than enough to do. After the war there was a flood of students anxious to make up for the time they had lost. They were not much younger than myself, and were perhaps the keenest and hardest-working generation I have known. The University had not really appreciated that greater numbers might require more staff. I taught the origins of the Spanish theatre, Latin American history and Camões, but had to supervise students who wanted all manner of things. It was excellent training and I have never regretted it. Before I started the course on the origins of the Spanish theatre, Trend gave me tea at a restaurant. I left my text in the restaurant, and he improvised for me while I went to recover it. I had a small but keen group for Camões: I knew nothing about the Prince of Poets, having in Portugal devoted myself (like Camões in India) to Portuguese history. We took turns to continue and comment on the octaves. My senior pupil was old Dr Rous, former headmaster of the Perse School and editor of the Loeb Classics. He attributed any non-Latin words to the influence of Sanskrit. He would arrive by bicycle, with a battered attaché-case containing his rations from which he detached his *Lusiads*. When it was not his turn he would doze off, being a little vexed with himself if we roused him and with us if we let him slumber.

My Spanish was far from perfect, and I was grateful for the help of Dr Batista i Roca, who spent his exile in England in promoting Catalan studies, for helping me with difficult proses. Spanish teachers were few, and I found myself supervising for a number of colleges as well as my own. Students expected an hour a week each, or at most two together, and had to be given a start on any relevant subject. I suppose I was expected to obtain a fellowship, but Spanish was a minor subject, and if colleges could obtain my services without, there was no particular reason why they should offer me one. Portuguese was an 'Other Language' and had no established post. Two members of the Spanish department had been seconded for government work, and it was their absence that caused my problem.

Probably, the department wanted me to reach a decision. I must have told Trend, for I have a note from him which begins 'this is rather serious: if we aren't careful we shall be faced with 'either' 'or',' and asking me to talk it over with Saunders. One solution would be to make me a part-time lecturer, which the General Board might not accept. There were two considerations to bear in mind: there was a man in residence who might more or less fill the bill, though he did not know Spanish as well as I did and had no Portuguese. Would the Foreign Office job continue, if so, I would get a higher salary than I would at Cambridge for many years to come.

A Memoir

PART SIX

IN THE SUMMER OF 1947 I decided to leave Cambridge and return to London. We discussed the sale of our house and I went in search of one in London. It seemed natural to try Hampstead first. I had to report to Ann that I could find no suitable house in Hampstead for less than three thousand pounds. We added a little to the asking price for the house in Cambridge. Ann suggested if not Hampstead, then Richmond. The situation there was not much better, but over the river in Twickenham an agent showed me a house near Strawberry Hill and Sandycombe Lodge, once the property of J.M.W. Turner, R.A. It was being used as shadow-factory, where women made airmen's mitts and helmets. Each room had its quota of heavy industrial sewing-machines: the vibration had shaken the plaster and it scarcely resembled a home. Permits were required for almost everything, and prospective buyers were probably frightened off by the dilapidated aspect of the house and the risks involved. Ann brought her sister Dorothy, recently back from Canada, and her two children. Ann would have left the decision to me. I asked Dorothy, who observed with her Canadian accent: 'Well, I guess it could be made budaful!' I took this as a challenge. We moved in September, with decorators and plasterers working round us. Turner had worked in an architect's office and had supervised the building himself. The house was perfectly sound. The two wings had been raised a floor in the later nineteenth century. The Italian marble mantelpiece in the dining-room had been broken and some new stairs were needed. Otherwise, most of the work was decoration. The staircase had been marbled. In 1947 there was nobody available who did marbling, for which I do not much care: it had to be papered. It is not often that a house built by a great painter – 'the genius of the age' – to his own design and for his own residence is found. It was and is unique. Ann was enchanted by it. Ann's first article on this then forgotten masterpiece appeared in *Country Life* in 1951, entitled 'Sandycombe Lodge: Turner's Little house in Twickenham.'

My history of Portugal was at length published by Cambridge in 1947. My return to the Foreign Office led to my being appointed secretary to Sir John Wise's mission to Brazil. At the end of the war Britain owed Brazil a considerable sum of money for goods bought on credit. The economic and financial mission had the task of negotiating how the debt should be paid and how post-war trade should be conducted. Sir John was a former governor of Burma, and his team consisted of representatives of the Treasury, Bank of England and Board of Trade and myself. The Foreign Office was aware that negotiations were unlikely during Carnival, so we set off the day after the festival. In fact, Rio de Janeiro takes time to recover from the exertions. The Foreign Office also supposed that a couple of weeks would suffice to settle the matters in hand. We met the President, General Dutra, who had been Getulio Vargas' minister for War, and many politicians, whom our opposite numbers had to satisfy. My appendix finally blew up and had to be removed. Our Brazilian friends were extremely attentive. I was privileged to meet the poet Manuel Bandeira in his charming house in the Largo do Boticário. I convalesced in a cottage attached to the Embassy's summer residence at Petrópolis. It was May when we finally took our aeroplane. The unexpectedly prolonged absence and my illness must have placed some strain on Ann in her new home, but we learned a useful lesson, that we could cope with such separations.

I suppose I wanted to get back into an educational setting. I was an established civil servant, but had no guarantee that I should not be posted to some part of the world in which my interest would be irrelevant. The workings of 'personnel departments' are quite mysterious. I was interested when a vacancy occurred for the educational director of the Hispanic and Luso-Brazilian Councils. The two-headed body was founded by a group of businessmen led by Lord Davidson, an Aberdonian ex-minister. It was registered as a charity because it existed to further educational and cultural relations with the Spanish and Portuguese-speaking countries. Its academic mentor had been Professor Allison Peers, who had considered leaving his chair to occupy the post, but last-minute differences had arisen and he had returned to Liverpool. I had the good fortune to be recommended by

Edward Wilson, who had succeeded Trend at Cambridge, was appointed and embarked on a rather hectic career of activity. Our premises were a former private house in Portman Street. It had a large dining-room suitable for entertaining, meetings and even exhibitions. The first floor housed the library in front, and the education department behind, three or four of us crowded in a single room. From here we organized language courses, the Portuguese at King's College, lectures, meetings and concerts. Ann naturally played and sang her part.

Under the auspices of the educational department, she gave recitals followed by the showing of a Spanish or Argentine film. The Greater London Council kindly lent its large auditorium at County Hall, which held a couple of thousand people, largely pupils or students. In Liverpool, the active Spanish society obtained the support of the director of education for a similar programme. In October 1949, the film was of Calderon's *La dama duende* made in Argentina. It was the era of Perón, and Evita had enlivened the Argentine embassy with three 'labour attaches', one a former head of the jockeys' union and one a petroleum worker. They expressed a desire to accompany us, more, to drive us, to Liverpool. My superior, a former ambassador, feared that they desired to use the occasion to make speeches, possibly inflammatory, with what dire results? I reassured him. We drove to Liverpool, stopping at Lichfield. The programme, in the Philharmonic Hall, went off well, with a thousand pupils from the Liverpool high-schools admitted free. The labour attaches were photographed on the stage with Ann and her bouquet and the dignitaries of Liverpool. I am sure that several copies were at once sent off to Evita and won her approval. It was a form of propaganda even I could condone.

The last programme for which we could afford the services of Ivor Newton was of Portuguese songs, for a Portuguese week in 1954. Ann prefaced her songs with an explanation. The following text will give some idea of her method:

The first three songs have been chosen to form a triptych of Portuguese womanhood – portraits in musical miniature. First, the young girl unconsciously displaying her innocent vanity, proud of her new blouse and determined to dance with her hair unbound despite her mother's equal determination that her daughter shall conform to the customs of her own young days. There is a mood of spontaneity and touches of ironical humour ... The melody is of special interest in its link with tunes still to be found in some country districts between Alicante and Valencia, and has something in common with the rare examples of the jota in two-four time ... The second song is of entirely different colour, dark, dramatic, passionate, the expression of the woman who has known the pleasure of love and now experiences its sorrows and disillusionment, but still bears traces of ironical observation even in grief ... The third picture is a little jewel of primitive art and typifies with gentle simplicity the 'ternura' of motherhood ... This melody from Arganil bears the patina of antiquity ... The next song, *canção de romaria,* is probably even older, note the primitive compass of five notes: it would be difficult to find a more unpretentious melody, yet it has a mysterious power more than many a large-scale rhapsody ... The anonymous artists and craftsmen of a country have certain basic principles in common, and the popular music of Portugal, like its bold pottery designs and glowing embroidery have all the decorative charm of a people gifted with the instinct for the embellishment of life.

Ann was feminine and would, I think, have regarded feminism as a solecism. She enjoyed giving her recitals of popular music to Women's Institutes and similar bodies. A photograph from the *Darlington and Stockport Times* shows her with the ladies of the committee in 1956. In October 1950 she accompanied me on our first visit to the United States. It was the sesquicentenary of the Library of Congress, and Lewis Hanke, an eager beaver if ever there was one, as director of the Hispanic Foundation organized the first Luso-Brazilian Colloquium, drawing together participants in many disciplines and from many parts of the world. Professor Charles Boxer, the eminent historian of the Portuguese in the East and of Brazil (whose funeral I attended yesterday, May 8, 2000) inaugurated the Greenlee collection on the Portuguese expansion in the Newberry Library in Chicago. From France came Professor Charles Aubrun and his wife Hilda, then of Bordeaux and later of the Institut Hispanique in the Sorbonne, who became friends for life. And many more. We landed in New York on Columbus Day, October 12, the anniversary of the discovery. It was a public holiday and the banks were shut. We had to stay on the quay until rescued. Hanke had arranged for our invitation to be extended by the University of California at Berkeley, so we obtained round-trip tickets which took us to Chicago, Seattle, Berkeley, the Grand Canyon, New Mexico, Texas, Mississippi, and Nashville, where our money again gave out and we had to take the night-train to Washington. We were entertained for Christmas at Beacon Street in Boston and then returned.

It was at this time that Ann wrote or completed these *Scenes from Spanish Life*. A note on the typescript bears the date San Francisco 1950. We were there in November. An internal reference shows that the period they describe was twenty years earlier. I went with her when she left them with a prominent New York agent whose office walls were covered with photographs of then celebrated authors they managed, one of them bearing the footnote 'with ten percent of all my love.' Evidently, I did not miss the ten per cent then or later. The *Scenes* are very English. Ann set them aside and they remained forgotten. The table of contents shows that two are missing, both on Andalusia, called 'Little Luz of Málaga' and 'Rose of Granada.' The second was an account of a visit to Falla. Searches have been made among her papers, and I kept the typescript for some time in the hope that the lacking pages would turn up. They have not done so, and her family agrees with me that there is no point in delaying publication any longer. The visit to Falla would have been of special interest. She said that Falla, who, like Turner, was a small man, had a large piano in a resonant bare room, which may account for some of his effects, and that he was cared for by his sister, Maria del Carmen. He left Barcelona for Buenos Aires in October 1939. He had been invited to participate in four programmes of Spanish music in which Conchita Badia sang to a full and enthusiastic audience, which must have erased any memories of Cambridge. Since 1926, he had devoted his life to his choral epic *L'Atlántida,* unfinished when he died, still attended by his sister, on November 14, 1949.†

Ann did not sing in the United States, though she made some musical friends. At Berkeley she met Joaquin Nin-Culmell, the son of Joaquin Nin, and professor of music in the University of California: his Tonadas, or transcriptions of Spanish folksongs for piano, were composed in 1956 to 1961. My history of Portugal was awarded a

---

† Although Falla was born in Cádiz and the settings major works were Andalusian, his father was a Valencian businessman and his mother a Catalan pianist. *L'Atlántida* sprang from the epic poem of Verdaguer in Catalan, which Falla edited for his choral epic. His object was to find a music to embrace all the styles of the Spanish provinces in a single musical work, a difficult if not impossible ambition.

prize, and early in 1950 we went to Lisbon to receive it. In Portugal, Ann renewed friendships made earlier and was invited to sing, an invitation she was now able to reciprocate. Our musicologist friend Santiago Kastner taught at the Lisbon Conservatoire: he had published his *Cravistas portugueses* at Mainz in 1935, and this was followed by his *Contribución al estudio de la música española y portuguesa* (Lisbon 1941) and monographs on Carlos de Seixas (1704–1742) and Frederico Mompou (Madrid 1947). He wrote to Ann in 1945 that he found many modern composers guilty of trickery and full of difficulties, but lacking in deep and true emotion, and so in humanity. He sought in vain the sobriety, simplicity and transcendental depth of Monteverdi or Purcell's *Dido and Aeneas*. 'So I play less modern music now, but I am always faithful to the ancients,' adding 'How I would like to make music with you, accompany your singing and work on repertory!'

We were able to put together a festival week in 1951, and weeks for Portugal, Mexico and Spain. That of June 1951 included an exhibition of drawings by Gregorio Prieto of places connected with Queen Isabella I for the centenary of her birth in 1451, a lecture by Ortega y Gasset and a short anthology of Spanish music with Eduardo Torner, the collector of Spanish popular songs, then an exile in London, using his *Cancionero musical español*. Ortega was entertained to lunch with Arnold Toynbee, T.S. Eliot, the aged medievalist Gómez Moreno, who happened to be in London, and Xavier de Salas, later director of the Prado. I had asked Ortega to speak about the *Revolt of the Masses*, (first published in 1930) twenty years on. I did not listen to his discourse, having engaged a recorder to make a tape of it. We ran the cable under the carpet, and when the talk was over the technician informed me rather crest-fallen that his apparatus had failed to work. Torner was an exceptionally timid man from the Asturias: when we invited him to dine he was in a state of nerves, and as the guests sat down asked me when were the 'other Spaniards' coming. He relaxed when I told him that he was on friendly ground and that there were no 'other Spaniards.'

Kastner generously dedicated his book on Seixas to Dr Ivo Cruz, director of the conservatory as the 'pioneer in the renascence of Portuguese music, and instigator of the reassessment of Portuguese music.' Ann regretted not being able to follow her history of Spanish music with an account of Portuguese, then unpublished: she remarked that you can't write about music unless you can hear it. Ivo Cruz and his wife came to London in July 1952, bringing an excellent pianist and teacher, Maria Cristina Lino Pimentel. The programme included some of his settings of Camões, and on his return he thanked me, asking me to convey to Ann his 'gratitude for her collaboration, his admiration for her art in singing, intelligence and cultivated taste with which she greatly enhanced my music.' He did not fail to mention their visits to Turner's house.

The fees we were able to pay were negligible. We could rarely afford the services of the brilliant Ivor Newton. In 1953 he played for a programme of new South American music. The young Argentine violinist Alberto Lysy, winner of the Queen of the Belgians' award and soon associated with Yehudi Menuhin, performed music by the Peruvian composer Armando Guevara, then in London, with Newton, who accompanied Ann in songs by Villalobos, Camargo Guarnieri and Guastavino. I think Villalobos was little known in Britain when Ann wrote a notice of him, calling him a whale among minnows, a phrase hardly more tactful than Fulford Williams' allocution. She acquired an array of modern Argentine composers. Armando Guevara departed for New York, writing that his partita was having 'a wonderful acceptance' and that Alberto's record was really outstanding. He added that Ann was right: she had been the first to judge it.

My most enduring friendship was with the Irish-Argentine writer Patricio Gannon: it dates from 1953 or 1954 and lasted till his death in March 1977. Patricio had a small estancia in Entre Rios and a flat in Buenos Aires, but feared chest infections and came every (European) summer to avoid the raw River Plate winter and to enjoy the attractions of Europe, 'one of which, and not the least, was my visits to Turner's house in Twickenham. What a delightful place Twickenham is! Nothing would stop me from settling down in a neat little house in Twickenham but the winter and my fears of chest complaints. By selling the estancia and cows I could easily do it, but the old estancia and the cows have their attractions.' Patricio was a devotee of English literature of the nineties, of Dowson (whose letters he collected) and Beardsley. One of his missions was to obtain the complete works of R.B. Cunninghame Graham for the institute at the small town of Gualeguaychú associated with the visits to the River Plate of Garibaldi and Cunninghame Graham. He asked how much it would cost to get the works: I replied ten pounds. We combed the six-penny trays and he took back twenty-three of them.

My favourite indulgence was to have devised the quarterly of Hispanic Studies called *Atlante*. We racked our brains for a title suitable to cover the whole area to which we were devoted. Sr Terrádez, a Spanish exile we had set up to manage a book-club, thought of *Atlante*. Ann contributed one essay, an article on Portuguese opera in the eighteenth century (1953) and an unsigned memoir of Eduardo Torner, who died in February 1955. Born at Oviedo in 1888, he had studied in Paris with D'Indy. His Cancionero of Asturias was one of the earliest regional collections: his last work was *Ensayos de estilistica literaria* (Oxford 1954): 'those who knew him will always remember his shy and self-effacing charm, the spark of enthusiasm which any reference to Spanish popular verse or music brought to his face, and the humour which he often referred to the foibles of his fellow-Asturians.'

In 1952 Ann contributed the sections on music for *Portugal and Brazil,* edited by W.J. Entwistle and myself as a memorial to Edgar Prestage, the first English professor of Portuguese, and, as it turned out, to Aubrey Bell, whose *Portuguese Literature* was the standard work on the subject in English, and who died, a refugee from the war, in British Columbia while the book was in preparation.

The pace could hardly last. Ann and I were both born in London and both hated its traffic. I had a small car, but the journey from Twickenham consumed much time. I rarely got to the British Museum. I had been consulted about a United Nations project to advance the cause of peace and culture by translating all the world's literature into all the world's languages. The member states had been asked to produce lists. The Dominican Republic produced a list of fifty, headed by the novel *Enriquillo*, translated by Robert Graves and checked by me. The originators of this ambitious plan had imagined that publishers would leap to collaborate if the cost of translation were met. They were mistaken. My advice was sought, and I suggested that it might be better to draw up an independent list. I was asked for suggestions and proposed the *Royal Commentaries of the Incas* of Garcilasso 'the Inca', the first great work in Spanish by an author of American indigenous birth, and therefore the inauguration of Castilian as an international language. I was then asked to undertake the task. The English part of the whole scheme passed to the American universities and my

version of the Inca appeared in two volumes from Texas with an intro-
duction by Arnold Toynbee in 1966.

The Councils had now moved from Portman Street to a more fash-
ionable building in Belgrave Square, which tempted the directors to
spend more on entertainment. The Councils no longer put funds
aside. Nor could I. I was now forty. When Hilda Finberg told Ann
that there was a Turner going for a hundred pounds, I had to say that
I could not spare a hundred pounds. One day while driving my small
Ford car from Sandycombe Lodge to Belgrave Square – or rather
while waiting for the traffic-lights to change – I fell to calculating how
much of my life I would waste in traffic jams. It came to over two
years. There was no chair going, at least anywhere they had a good
library and I wanted to go. We had no children, which, however
regrettable, freed us. I foresaw problems for Ann and myself. I left
Councils rather abruptly, and took refuge with my aunt and uncle,
devoting much time to the Inca, which Jack's wife kindly typed for
me. I then told Ann we would have to make a drastic change. I went
for a visit to Chicago, where the Newberry Library, then under the
benign rule of Stanley Pargellis, found a short term fellowship for me.
A vacancy occurred at Toronto, but it was for Spanish with Italian,
which I did not have: it went to Geoffrey Stagg, a Cambridge con-
temporary. I then wrote to the University of British Columbia, which
was in full expansion under Norman Mackenzie. It had a department
of Romance Languages, and Professor J.G. Andison wrote me a cor-
dial letter: he would be glad to have me, but anything above assistant
professor would be exceptional. I had only a vague idea what an
assistant professor was, and did not much care: I had no idea that I
would take to Vancouver and spend my time there until I retired. I
told Ann, who was probably rather more shaken than she showed.
Once more I set off alone to prospect.

A Memoir

PART SEVEN

MY DEPARTURE FROM THE COUNCILS AFFECTED Ann's singing career, but only to some extent.

Edward Wilson recommended me to Andison with generous warmth, attributing my defection from the Councils to my desire to maintain academic standards, which was the part of the truth that concerned them both. Ann's sister Dorothy was the widow of a Canadian soldier and had returned from Manitoba with her two half-Canadian children. It was as well that I went alone to Vancouver, for I did not know how Ann would take the change and the accommodation at the University of British Columbia was very different from Sandycombe Lodge. Andison and others were helpful, and I was able to arrange something better when Ann arrived. We soon found an excellent, large and light flat on the endowment lands. I had not imagined that we would remain in Vancouver until I retired. This was made possible by the short academic year, which allowed us to be at Sandycombe Lodge from May until September. As Ann still distrusted aeroplanes, we crossed the Atlantic in the *Queen Mary* or *Queen Elizabeth* and took the transcontinental train from Montreal or Toronto, or sometimes the American route by Chicago or Seattle. The transcontinental train, with its roomettes, its dome-car from which to observe the Rockies under the stars, and its excellent restaurant-car, crossed Canada in five days, making eleven with the sea-voyage, little more than the daily ordeal of crossing London, and a great deal pleasanter: one could read and write on the great liners and in the roomettes. After the seamen's strike of 1968, the Atlantic crossing ceased to be viable, and Ann adapted herself at last to the aeroplane.

Forty-odd years ago Vancouver was a provincial city with one bookshop and one auditorium which served for visiting circuses, for boxing, and, with the ropes removed, for the visits of the Amadeus.

Under the premiership of W.A.C. Bennett, a hardware merchant from Kelowna and his Social-Crediters, it was beginning to boom. An Austrian immigrant named Koerner brought wealth to the forestry industry and benefited the University. Millions of salmon were born in the Fraser and other rivers. The immigrants from Europe, if not quite so prolific, brought delicatessen, Robsonstrasse and some good students to UBC.

Ann gave only one concert in Vancouver. She had not looked for an accompanist and was already immersed in Turner and other studies. The piano and her collection of music were for the months we spent at Sandycombe Lodge. Her 'explorations' of literary territory accompanied her reading, which was constant and wide-ranging. Her article on Gil Vicente and Shakespeare appeared in Reginald Horrocks' *Book Handbook* in 1951. I doubt if she seriously pretended that Shakespeare read the father of the Portuguese theatre, who died in 1536, but whose collected plays were printed only in 1562, two years before Shakespeare's birth: his *Jubileu d'amor* was certainly performed in 1531 at Brussels, where it scandalized the Nuncio and Cardinal Aleandro, and Aubrey Bell had posed the problem in 1921.

I cannot vouch exactly for dates. If Ann were given a diary, either it remained in mint condition or she covered the pages with notes on Mozart or whatever she was thinking about, ignoring days, months and even lines. Mine were laconic: BM meant I spent part of the day at the British Museum; a name or place might recall someone or somewhere; 'doctor' may mean that either Ann or I was ill. During the fifties, she was immersed in Turner. Her closest friend was Hilda Finberg, widow of A.J. Finberg, author of the standard *Life of J.M.W. Turner, R.A.* (Oxford 1939). A.J., who, like Turner, was born on St George's day, had in 1905 been entrusted by the Trustees of the National Gallery with the task of sorting out the 'massive chaos' of the Turner papers. Eleven tin boxes were as Ruskin left them in 1858. Finberg catalogued 19,331 items of the Bequest. He died in March 1939, just before his biography was published. Hilda kept for a time their large house in Barnes. She devoted herself to the revision of her husband's book, but she was learned about many other matters. She wrote of the eighteenth-century Jewish families in Twickenham and formed a very large collection of topographical prints, which passed to the Richmond Museum. She gave up the house at Barnes, and took a flat in St Margaret's very close to us. She died in December 1958,

while we were in Canada. Ann deeply regretted the loss of this devot-
ed scholar, with her sharp eye and quiet manner, and at her instiga-
tion the Turner Society held a session in Hilda's honour at the Royal
Academy under the chairmanship of Sir Hugh Casson on St George's
day 1983.

Ann probably met Hilda through Edward Croft-Murray, the keep-
er of prints and drawings at the British Museum, who had thought of
buying Sandycombe for his old mother, and who later wrote the
wording for the plaque on the house. Ann's own line of research was
more literary (and musical). She published 'J.M.W. Turner's
Unknown Verse-book' in the *Connoisseur Year-book* for 1957. The
verse-book contained no drawings and had therefore been allocated
to Turner's next-of-kin. Michael Kitson, the most accomplished of
art-historians, wrote in his obituary of Ann: 'Ann Livermore drew
attention to the book and published part of its contents. This article
was, however, far more than a piece of dedicated antiquarianism.
With her acute intelligence and enquiring scholarly mind, she saw
that the writing of poetry, for all the artist's lack of facility with
words, was an important clue to Turner's approach to painting. As
she put it, 'Not only is Turner's choice of subject-matter involved, but
also the temper of mind in which he moulded his impressions.' Such
a view is nowadays almost a commonplace, but at the time Ann
Livermore formulated it Turner was generally held to be a great artist
despite, not because of, his interest in literary matter. But her critical
mind went further than that, and in a direction not so widely fol-
lowed up since, though it surely ought to be.' Ann's knowledge of
James Thomson (himself a resident of Richmond) and his *Seasons,*
allowed her to perceive that Turner was profoundly influenced by
Thomson, not only as a poet but also in his choice of subjects for his
paintings. She was a pioneer in another way, the first to apply the
methods of iconology to Turner's work.

Ann's other essays on Turner included 'Turner and children' and
'Turner and Music' (*Music and Letters,* 1957, reprinted in *Turner
Studies,* vol. 3 1983). Kitson noted that Turner wrote out quite pro-
fessionally most of the basic musical signs, including a couple of
scales and even essayed a few melodies: he also apparently played the
flute. '1808 was also the year, or approximately the year, when he
composed at least two short poems in praise of music, poems which
are among his most successful. His imagination was captivated by

music, although the way he responded to it, that is by jotting down practical notes about it, was perhaps more of a piece than Ann Livermore realised with the way he responded to anything that came within his view.'

In the sixties Ann's time was divided between Vancouver and Sandycombe Lodge. On returning to England at the close of the academic term, we took out the car and drove to Madrid and Lisbon, before returning to London and Vancouver. We visited the Institut Hispanique in the Sorbonne, of which Charles Aubrun was director until the student riots of 1968. In Madrid, we visited Joaquin Rodrigo and his wife Victoria Kamhi. I had met Rodrigo through organizing a course in Madrid for English teachers of Spanish. The audience, not particularly musical, was fascinated by his pleasing voice and gentle smile: dark glasses concealed his sightlessness and he deftly manipulated the apparatus that played his scores. Federico Sopeña had published a short biography in 1946, when he was appointed professor of the history of music in Madrid. He was then unknown in Britain. One of the students remarked that he had no idea that a composer of such ability existed in Spain – Falla had died in Argentina in November 1946. He played his songs to Ann when we visited the flat in Madrid, and he laughingly referred to her as his 'maja inglesa.' When he and Victoria came to London they stayed at Sandycombe Lodge. Ann's far-ranging studies in art and literature blossomed in the sixties. In 1960 she was invited to collaborate in the commemoration of the centenary of Velázquez's death. The *Varia Velasqueña* consisted of two large volumes, the first on the painter's life and work, and the second of essays on his times. Ann chose to write about the philosopher Francisco Sánchez, whose 'De ... universali scientia quod nihil scitur' was first printed in 1581. Ortega y Gasset, writing in 1950, had compared Velázquez with Descartes, the two living in 'dramatic solitude,' immune from the intellectual conventions of the time: Descartes had reduced thinking to reason, and Velázquez reduced painting to the visible. Velázquez said nothing about anything. Ann pointed out that Descartes could not have had any formative influence on Velázquez, but that Sánchez was born at Tuy in the time of Velázquez's father: his argument was that the only way to study anything was through objects themselves. Past masters of science had used their imagination, and offered a tapestry of fables and fictions. Sánchez writes as a doctor, and discussed light and sight.

Velázquez's pupils came to study how to paint real objects, not to learn theory.

The article impressed the historian and social philosopher Luis Díez del Corral, who wrote:

'a work as subtle as Ann's would do honour to any publication in which it appeared. This is not my judgement, but that of someone much more qualified than myself, Lafuente Ferrari, which should please her. Lafuente was sorry not to have known earlier of her work on Velázquez and F. Sánchez so as to have drawn on her ideas, which he found extremely interesting ... Lafuente struggles against the narrow pedantry (*eruditismo*) by which many of his colleagues are confined. Studies like Ann's do not abound in this country.'

By now Ann had passed on to a study of Goya and Feijó in response to a request from Hernani Cidade, then literary editor of *Colóquio* in Lisbon, who sought the approval of his arts colleague, Reynaldo dos Santos. Another attempt to show the connection between a painter and ideas prevailing in his time was her essay on Rembrandt and Jansen, which appeared in *Apollo* in April 1967. A tattered list names a dozen essays published in these years, some with the note 'written in Canada,' or 'Vancouver.' They appeared in the *Quarterly Review*, the *Downside Review*, the review of Comparative Literature in Paris and the *Bulletin* of the French Institute in Portugal.

Patricio Gannon, from his cultural metropolis, affected to believe that British Columbia did not exist, unless as a 'gold-rush place like the one in *Rose Marie*' (he was not much given to music but doted on 'musicals'). He imagined that its professors looked like mounted police, though he conceded that he was probably wrong. In a bookseller's catalogue he came across 'Mr Livermore's Dream' by Sir Arthur Pinero. 'I cannot guess what Mr L.'s dream was, but I can very well imagine that Mrs L.'s dream is that of being back at the pleasance of the Sandycombe estate as soon as possible.' When I visited him at the estancia called Las Perdices or, on his stationery, San Juan de la Cruz, in December 1966, he thought Ann 'immensely wise in staying at the Elysian fields of Twickenham.' He introduced me to Borges, Mallea and his other friends, and showed me the Recoletos and the institute at Gualeguaychú, but Ann never went to South America. Patricio published his book of travel in Greece, his *Pausanias*, which won a couple of prizes, and set himself the congenial task of interviewing the illustrious and aged, Max Beerbohm,

Bertrand Russell, Santayana, Gordon Craig and others. He finished the collection in 1972, and called it *Cráneos Privilegiados* (I believe the reference is to Rubén Darío).

At the University of British Columbia, Spanish had prospered. When Andison retired, it became a separate department, one of the largest in the Commonwealth. This owed something to the reluctance of British Columbians to learn French (which French?), but more to a requirement for all students to do two years of a foreign language, which should of course have been done in high-school. This done, the case would have become normal, but for Mr Trudeau's attempt to impose bilingualism, i.e. French, which restored the status quo. Graduate studies were developed, and soon overdeveloped; the needs of the province were met, and it was not (in my view) our function to provide Ph. D.'s for export. We might never become an outstanding department, and in those years of general expansion we were usually in search of staff, but for our (Ann's and my) purposes, the combination of long terms, adequate library funds, a tolerable climate, with no question of citizenship or of giving up Sandycombe Lodge, worked well enough. We stayed. The unrest of 1968 obliged us to give up the great transatlantic liners and take to the air, but we escaped the turmoil which beset the Sorbonne, obliging Charles Aubrun to accept a chair at Nice created for him, a thing then unknown in French academic life.

On getting back to Sandycombe, we used to take out the car and drive through France, visiting the Aubruns, to Madrid and so to Lisbon, before returning to London for July and August. Barcelona was too far for visiting, and Ann no longer kept up her friendships there. However it was at Barcelona that the Spanish version of her *Short History of Spanish Music* was published in 1976. She was asked to write this for Duckworth in London by Lord Horder, either at the suggestion of Mosco Carner, the biographer of Puccini, or Eric Blom, the editor of *Music and Letters* and editor of Grove. It was written in some haste to meet a now forgotten deadline. A publisher's flyer shows that it was ready in August 1972, just before we returned to Canada. The review in the *Daily Telegraph* noted that 'the book is written from a deep knowledge and love of Spain and Spanish music, and shows an ability to recognise the main lines of development underlying the often puzzling variety of detail in each age.' The critic observes that Ann had known Spain and Spanish musical life for some forty years, and that she concerned herself exclusively with music as a discipline *per se* rather than in a social context. He appreciated her praise of Felipe Pedrell, whose researches provided a ground for such completely different personalities as Albéniz, Turina, Granados and Falla. I have no memory of the circumstances and have found no diary for the year, but I recall stopping on our way to Madrid and Lisbon at Steep in Hampshire where Mervyn Horder had built a sort of concrete bunker on a stream as a summer hideout within sight of the nursing-home once owned by his father, the royal physician.

The year 1973 marked the sixth-hundredth anniversary of the Anglo-Portuguese Alliance. I was asked to contribute to a booklet for the occasion, and the Portuguese President was invited to a service in St George's Chapel and a lunch given by the Queen at Windsor. I was somehow elected to the Lisbon Academy of Science, and in June Ann accompanied me to Lisbon. My talk on the first English historian of Portugal, the author of *De expugnatione Lyxbonensi*, was printed, undeservedly, since I had not then identified 'R' as Raol. St George is, of course, the patron of Lisbon.

Turner came into his own with the celebration of the bicentenary of his birth on April 23 1775. Ann had been gently but persistently pressing the case of the painter from Sandycombe Lodge since 1948. She was not one to take an aggressive stand, but would have understood when Henry Moore, then chairman of the newly founded Turner Society, declared in a letter to the *Times* that after Shakespeare Turner was England's greatest asset. She herself was steeped in both. The bicentenary was also the starting-point for the movement to fulfil Turner's wish that there should be a Turner Gallery. It was realized by the building of the gallery adjoining the Tate with funds from the estate of Sir Charles Clore. By 1980 plans had been approved and the gallery was opened by the Queen-Mother on April 19 1983. In 1986 the Prince of Wales became patron of the Society. As long ago as 1900 it had been agreed that a commemorative plaque should be placed on St Paul's church in Covent Garden, where Turner's parents were married in August 1773, where he was baptized and where his sister, who died at the age of eight, was buried. For reasons unknown to me it was never affixed. The Greater London Council decided to place one of their Wedgwood plaques on Sandycombe Lodge. This was done in 1977. I had been hesitant to agree, fearing lest during our long absences it should attract thieves, not without reason, for a break-in occurred in July 1977. The culprit was later caught, and proved to have been on parole after serving half of a seven-year sentence: at Kingston Crown Court he was given a suspended sentence and thus enabled to resume his activities. There was consequently no ceremony when the plaque was inaugurated.

Patricio Gannon died in March 1977. He had finished the *Cráneos Privilegiados* in 1972, and in 1973 Ann had an operation in Vancouver. Her sister Margaret came to look after her while I paid a shortened visit to Europe. Patricio sent Ann a card from Valldemosa showing Chopin's room, and met me in Twickenham. Sir Eugen Millington Drake, who had been the British representative in Uruguay at the time of the Graf Spee affair, had maintained his attachment to the River Plate and endowed the Hudson Institute in London, later merged into the Hispanic and Luso-Brazilian Councils. In 1966, during my visit, he was in Uruguay and Buenos Aires. He had once rowed in the Boat Race, but in his old age was bent with arthritis. My last sight of him was when I was driving down Piccadilly and avoided killing him as he awkwardly scuttled across the road. Patricio was entrusted with the task of composing a biography, his 'job in hand' as he wrote in May 1975. Patricio came to London for a meeting of the P.E.N. and collected material from the many sources associated with Sir Eugen. He also visited my cousins near Málaga. When he returned to Buenos Aires, he wrote up the memoir and gave it to an English lady to type. He returned by taxi with the manuscript and typescript. He must have left both in the taxi. He got up suddenly in the night, and the cleaner found him on the floor of his apartment when she arrived early next morning. He lingered a few days, but the stroke was fatal. I believe the typescript were never found.

I retired from the University of British Columbia in 1980. I had become involved in a contest to defend the rights of a head to deny permanent employment to those who were less than competent. Those in charge were unwilling to risk backing me and suggested that I resign. This I refused to do, and suggested they might prefer to dismiss me. I had nothing to lose, since I was on the verge of retirement and might have won an appeal. But Ann took the affair more to heart than I. Later, both tenure and permanent heads of department were done away with at UBC. There was some delay in finding a suitable successor. When this was done, we left.

The Turner bicentenary in 1977 led to a new appreciation of the artist, 'England's greatest asset after Shakespeare'. For Ann, who was steeped in both, the placing of the plaque without any attendant fuss was repayment for her devotion to the painter and to Sandycombe Lodge. The guardianship of The Turner gallery at the Tate passed to Andrew Wilton, whose work was commended by Michael Kitson, the most discerning of art historians, as brilliant. It would be invidious to pick out those who have contributed most to what might be called the Turner revival, if the great man were ever dead. Many are recorded in *Turner Studies* and the *Turner Society News*. Ann's article on '*Turner and Music*' of 1957 was reprinted in *Turner Studies* in 1983. She did not I think publish any more on Turner. An article on 'Turner and the Sunrise' remains unpublished. In it she shows that it is not sunsets, as is often imagined, but sunrise, the source of light, that most inspired the 'impresario of dawn.'

We had left Vancouver in August 1980. I liked having a foot in both worlds, and we had thought to retain our apartment there. It soon became clear that Ann could no longer undertake the long flight. At one moment, she suggested, at some cost, that I return alone. I replied that this was not a solution. In May 1981, I returned to clear up the apartment and bring back our books, furniture and papers. My cousins joined me, and we drove over familiar scenes and travelled the length of Vancouver Island. I have cordial invitations to return, and regret that circumstances have not made it possible. We thought for a moment of acquiring a second home in Portugal, and went to Lisbon in June 1983 with this in mind, but Ann slipped on the hotel staircase and ricked her ankle. She was well looked after, and I visited the Azores for a conference on Camões, but house-hunting was out of the question, fortunately, since she would soon have been unable to travel. In the following year we went to an exhibition and conference on Turner in Wales at Llandudno, but travelled by train. Charles and Hilda Aubrun came to England every summer, staying at Folkestone. We drove down to lunch and strolled on the Lees with them, sometimes staying the night. We revisited the coast of Kent from St Margaret's Bay to Margate, including the village of Dymchurch, briefly famous in our annals.

As I type these words, Hilda Aubrun, who is now ninety-eight and no longer writes, telephones from St Germain, where she is in a home. I do not think this is mere telepathy (whatever that may be). Charles, an *officier* of the Legion of Honour, and Hilda were installed in the Legion's residence in the Château du Val at St Germain. They continued their annual visits to Folkestone until 1990, when the state of his heart made travel unadvisable. He was given a transplant in February 1993, and was recovering when I saw him in the British Hospital, but a few days later Hilda telephoned me to say that he had died. He was the most competent of the French Hispanists of his day.

Ann continued to visit Turner exhibitions in England, such as that at King's Lynn in 1986, where we passed pleasant days with Stanley Warburton, one of founders of the Turner Society and one of the most knowledgeable Turnerites, and his wife Sheila. Ann's zest for Turner continued unabated. She liked to drive almost daily round Richmond Park stopping at Kingston Hill for me to see Tom Girtin, the lineal descendant of Turner's Tom Girtin, confined to his room after a stroke. She also regularly visited her brother Jack who had had a similar misfortune. Perhaps her last journey was to Spalding in August 1990 for my cousin's birthday. After a certain amount of discussion about whether she could stay in a hotel or not, she finally elected to go there and back in a day and was full of vitality in the midst of a large and animated party.

Her book on Spanish art, named *Artists and Aesthetics in Spain,* appeared in 1988. She had at least two other projects. One was called *Love in Portugal.* An undated table of contents shows that it was to have four parts, one medieval, including Nun'Alvares and Sir Galahad and Queen Philippa and the Loyal Counsellor. The second was filled with Bernardim Ribeiro's *Livro das saudades* and Camões. A loose sheet found in one of her printed articles on Stendhal's *De l'amour* (which she admired) gives an outline of her thoughts on Ribeiro. His little book held a unique place in the hearts of generations because of its privileged insight into the process of falling into and out of love. Writing in the early sixteenth century, he deliberately chose to base much of his structure on love-poems of the thirteenth, 'transforming medieval verses into renaissance prose in delicate currents aroused by his own experience. His characters conform to what we know of the Reconquest period when women were kept behind walls and guarded as pawns in the conflicts of resettlement and ancient land and titular rights. The women, when they were able, resisted decisions that restrained or impoverished their means, privileges and choice, taking considerable risks if they transgressed the laws of normal marriage, and using every feminine weapon at hand at whatever cost.' There follows a 'miniature anthology of popular love-songs, 'Love in the Village,' and titles for ten sections on more modern themes, some recognizable as articles that had already appeared: 'Saudades in the Embassy' or Sir Benjamin Keene; 'Love in Blue Stockings,' or the Marquesa de Alorna; 'The Lover all Romantick,' or Almeida Garrett; 'Passion in Oporto,' or Camilo Castelo Branco; 'An Antidote,' Eça de Queiroz; and 'A Hamlet in Portugal,' the *Cartas de amor* of Fernando Pessoa.

Ann's other late interest was with the belief that Turner in his English travels had followed the routes given by Defoe. She combed the works of both for relevant details, which, instead of serving for an article, soon grew into a large book. Stanley Warburton helped her to try to get the result published. I am grateful for his solicitude, but I felt that this could be done only with a substantial subsidy, and that if by chance I were to predecease her, she would be left inadequately provided for. Signs of failing powers were evident. It required the services of several home helps to get her up and dressed. She ceased to be able to go out for her regular drive round Richmond Park and could eat only the few dishes I had learned to cook. As she had very little memory, she was content to enjoy what there was, regardless of repetition. Music remained with her. Her voice was steady and clear, and she would break out into a recital of carols in the middle of the night, even though she had forgotten the words. When Joseph Estorninho, the nephew of Carlos, my oldest Portuguese friend, first came to see her in 1994, he remarked that he had been told that she was a singer. She did not reply, but drew herself up in the chair to which she was confined and sang a loud high F, which she held until her breath gave out. She died two days after her birthday, in October 1995.

It is not for me to speak dispassionately of Ann or her life and work. Despite her travels and her international interests, she was as English as Elgar, or as Turner himself. In an obituary in the *Turner Society News*, Michael Kitson recalled visiting Turner's 'delightful small country villa near the Thames' in the seventies and thought it 'a civilized and friendly house, as suitable for modem occupiers as it must have been for Turner.' He thought that Ann's principal article on Turner was that on the unknown verse-book (1957), and praised her acute intelligence and enquiring scholarly mind. I have already cited his words: 'the writing of poetry, for all the artist's lack of facility with words, was an important clue to Turner's approach to painting'. Such a view is nowadays almost a commonplace, but at the time Ann Livermore formulated it, Turner was generally held to be a great artist despite, not because of his interest in literary matters. But the article went further than that, and in a direction not so widely followed up since, though it surely ought to be. Stanley Warburton added his own reminiscences, concluding with the mournful Sonnet 30, 'precious friends hid in death's dateless night'. It closes on a more consoling note:

> But if the while I think on thee, dear friend,
> All losses are restored and sorrows end.

23 April, St George's Day–23 May, 2000

Woman with a Parrot
AND
Old Man with a Canary

SHE LIVED IN THE LAST house along the bay. Unlike the other white villas, however, Teresa's home turned its back upon the encircling marine panorama which lay to the north-east. The owners of those other houses were seasonal visitants from the stale airlessness of Madrid and the torrid, panting, glaring South. Teresa lived here all the year round where for months at a time the north wind blew and shrieked its bleak, drear message, icily punctuated by the volleying hail-storms which enforced its unrelenting wilfulness. So her doors and the shuttered windows and balcony faced southwest, overlooking the sea-cliff sanctuary of San Roque where it jutted out upon a rocky ledge above the sea two hundred feet below.

But Teresa herself was indifferent to the elements of nature, clement or otherwise. She waged war, by a kind of self-instituted siege, on a world of humankind; no other form of living matter existed for her. There was the life of man; all else was 'muy bruto'. Certainly she would have stared to hear anyone idealise or personalise nature.

The lower slopes of the great pine cliffs encroached upon her court-yard at the rear. There was scarcely any clearing in the way and an umbrageous stillness hung low behind the foremost sentinels of the forest, as if asserting the authority of their right and title to the wildest sweeps of all that inaccessible and rocky northern coast. Only the lighthouse stood out as witness to the steadfastness of men. High and white, it towered on the topmost headland of the promontory.

There was no other dwelling on that ascent between Teresa's villa and the lighthouse, and for eight months of the year the rough mule-track through the pines was trodden only by the coastguard men and Guardias Civiles on periodical rounds of inspection. There was a goat-track which clung to the edge of the cliffs, but no goat was ever seen in that perilous place, and no man either – in daylight. In the short summer season a visit to the lighthouse was, of course, de rigueur, and donkeys carried up lunch and merienda for the visitors who could climb so far. A motor-track had long been mooted: but so far, no progress had been made. It had been one of the last projects of the dictator Primo, who had latterly bought a rough shooting-place a few kilometres further along, and only last year the first lev-elling had been made on the more or less easy slope some four hundred metres on the townward side of the sanctuary. But Primo had gone: King Alfonso turned uneasily in bed while his officials waited for a cue that never came; the contractors cancelled their con-tracts and the workmen were as idle as before. Though many feared it, only a few dared to believe that a miracle of change could take place and nobody ever suggested in words that this might prove the last *grande saison* of the monarchy. Yet so it was to be.

May had brought its annual truce; the battering-ram of wind and rain was withdrawn until September, and bolts, bars and barricades were cautiously taken down from the sanctuary villa. I had been sent up from the town below, about three kilometres away. Neither of the two commercial hotels in the long main square was suited for the long stay I wished to make and the grand barrack of a beach hotel was still shut. It would in any case have been beyond my means. But the priest who had once visited Ireland sent up a message to the Villa Heliotrope, as it was called, and by return of his messenger I was bid-den to merienda for the morrow.

This priest had already explained to me that Teresa was the guardian and overseer of the little shrine, which lay within the patronage of the King's aged aunt and that in the Villa Heliotrope were kept the vessels and garments pertaining to its cult. There was relatively little to do, for there was but one festival in the year, but since the Saint's Day fell during the month of the royal stay that func-tion had acquired almost the status of a national ceremony to which people crowded from far and near.

The villa was easily found, about a kilometre above the shuttle tram-way terminus shed. Entrance to the fore-court was barred by high, uncompromising iron gates, still locked, I noted, at half-past four on that spring afternoon. However, a constant watch on the out-side world was evidently kept, for I had only begun to fumble for some catch or other, when a little young man darted down the stone steps from the front door on the balcony and admitted me with reassuring smiles, inviting me to 'Advance! Advance! señorita!'.

At first sight Teresa seemed black and harsh. She was compact of all that racial severity which has nothing to do with the nervous irritability of more mobile peoples. She proffered nothing, she promised nothing. But her house was clean, though bare, and it was cleanliness I sought, so I bided my time and waited for her to make me an offer of accommodation, if willing to do so.

She was not young, but she was not old. She was not handsome, but neither was she ugly. There were no white streaks in the black hair she wore dragged back into a plaited ball high on her neck. But there were lines drawn more deeply from the corners of the nose to her mouth than a woman in her prime usually has to show. Her skin had an uncared-for sallow tinge, yet her eyes were bright and darting. She was quite small, her feet were arched and tiny and she walked in a peculiarly pushing manner taking short quick steps but pointing her toes outwards at an angle which may have been admired by a former generation, but nowadays attracts only ridicule except in remote, sedate centres of provincialism where its associations with a faded coquetry still echo round forgotten corners.

But there was no echo of coquetry in Teresa's voice and no sensation of remoter memories in its inflexion. She spoke with a harsh actuality of tone, as if goaded by the prick of continual reality. Yet it was plain at first sight that within herself she guarded an unbreakable will. There was nothing of the dove about her and little of the eagle. She resembled rather a solitary raven, withdrawn, or driven, from the flock.

'You are younger than I thought', she frowned at me after a while. I sat mute, since there was no appeal against that accusation.

'I have come to study,' I explained, after a minute's silence, during which we looked at one another.

'Yes. So I hear. Well, I suppose there is no mischief in that!' 'I hope not,' I replied. 'You have recently come from the Cathedral festival at Pamplona?' she went on, in the same tone of prosecutor and judge in one.

'That is so. I came from England to hear the Guerrero and Morales music.'

'You came all the distance from England to hear that?' She made it seem as if I had made some damaging admission of guilt. 'Why?'

'Because I have come to Spain to study music. I thought I could not make a better beginning than that, and I was right.' I spoke up more bravely for my own convictions than usual and she seemed to think better of me for doing so. But she only frowned the more.

'Music! But I thought it was for the language! Then why have you come here? You will find no academies, certainly no royal Conservatorios in San Roque.' She sounded personally displeased.

'We have too many academies in England. I know all about them.'

'But San Roque! We have no music here. You have wasted your time.' She spoke with such a forbidding aspect that I felt she meant that I was wasting her time, so I prepared to take my leave. But again I found myself speaking with a touch of assurance that was new. 'You may not know it, señora, but you have some excellent *coros* in the district – among the shepherds and fishermen, I have heard.'

'Oh, they are strong, idle fellows enough and I daresay they can fill their lungs to capacity as well as in any other part of Spain.'

'It's not so much that, señora, nor even because of the pretty turns of melodies and pleasant cadential tricks about here. If you will forgive my technical jargon, it is the instinct for organic form by which they string songs and interludes together that interests me quite genuinely.'

'And you have come here for that! You can truthfully say you have not wasted your time?' She was still incredulous, but a little curious now.

'No, certainly not! Already I have found plenty to do, only – it is very uncomfortable down there; dirty, and never quiet.'

'Ah! So you seek quiet, do you?'

'Well, yes! That is, when I am not making a noise myself, of course!' I looked to see if she would appreciate the mild joke at my own expense, but she made no sign of answering humour.

'And you want to be clean?'

'Si, señora! ' The fervency of these words made contact between us at last. But still she resisted me. 'Well, you can't stay down there. I suppose there is no remedy.' She did not move, however, so I got up.

'I have no wish to intrude, señora!' 'You are not intruding, señorita. I invited you to come. But it is the music, you see. That is an obstacle. I was not warned of it.'

'I am sorry. I did not know! One of the joys of coming to Spain has been my discovery that music is a key which opens many doors, of all kinds and conditions.'

At these words Teresa lifted and turned her head a little, as though listening for an echo. She waited as if to allow some inaudible sounds to die away, then opened her mouth to speak. For a moment no words came; but then she abruptly changed her mind and said something obviously opposed to what she had first meant involuntarily to say.

'There are doors and doors, señorita! Some of them you might come to wish you had never entered, that had never been opened to you, that you would have prayed to pass by, had you known where they might lead you.'

'I am sorry, very sorry,' I said at length, not knowing how to take this remark of hers. 'Probably you fear you might wish you had never opened your doors to me. I suppose I should be an annoyance to you, señora.'

'Oh, not to me!' she answered, quickly. 'That is all past and done with!' She reflected a moment severely, then with a brisker tone explained.

'But there is Anibal to think of.'

'Anibal?'

'The parrot!'

'Oh! The parrot! Anibal? I see.'

'He is incurably sensitive to sound, music especially. It irritates him unbelievably! '

'I am very sorry,' I said. 'Very sorry.' And again 'VERY sorry.'

Just then a canary near at hand burst into a flood of ecstatic joy. It was as if the sun was pouring forth its warmth and life in that constricted dwelling. 'Tio!' TIO!' she called harshly. 'Cover the cage! Cover the cage!'

There was a hasty shuffle behind a glass door which opened on to a small alcove out of the front sala. I saw the shadow of a human shape raise its arms. Then the canary was silent.

SQUAWK! SQUAWK! came a grating acknowledgement from some dark interior along the corridor to the back of the house.

'You see how it is?' Teresa enquired. Her eyes seemed more protuberant than I had noticed before as she searched my expression to see how exactly I comprehended the situation.

'Anibal is taking his siesta, I suppose?' I said with a smile.

'Yes. He is getting on, nobody knows how old he is, and he likes to sleep a full afternoon.'

'Your canary is a wonderful little singer. His notes are very true, so sweet!'

She drew her brows down a little on hearing this. 'To sing, though they put you in a cage! Would you do that? I call it foolish, myself! The canary is no bird of mine! It belongs to my uncle, my great uncle. Such stupid creatures! If they ceased to sing in captivity perhaps people would stop putting them in cages. You do not find such songs meaningless, then señorita?'

'It is the nature of the bird to sing, señora. And we are all in cages.'

'You, too? I should not have thought so!' She spoke ironically. 'For a young girl, you seem to move about the world with singular freedom!'

'I have only got out of my cage for a little while, señora. They will probably catch me yet! Who knows?' She stood up suddenly.

'Would you care to se the room?'

'Thank you. If – if I may ...' Her sudden capitulation took me by surprise.

At the door I halted. 'There is one matter, though. I want to hire a piano.'

'A piano! ' The battle of wills threatened to break out again. But here I stood my ground. A piano was indispensable to me.

'But where would you get a piano?'

'I was told to go to Fernández Viuva.'

'And who told you that? She is a shark! Viuva, indeed! Viuva! A convenient term, indeed! I will arrange that for you.'

'I need a good instrument,' I said firmly.

'Did you expect to get one there? I will see to it. They will not cheat anyone lodging in this house!'

'I am very much obliged to you' I said, not having been aware that Fernandez' widow or anyone else had had any intention of cheating me.

'Durango will be able to supply you, and he will send it up free of charge. I will see to that. And will you like this room?'

'Yes, indeed. But it will have to be a small piano.' I said, looking round the tiny bedroom.

'The piano can go in the dining-room.'

'But would that not disturb Anibal? Here it would be more out of the way, would it not?'

'So long as you do not perform during the afternoon. He spends the morning on the veranda, unless it is very cold. Perhaps you could arrange to use the instrument more in the morning?'

'By all means. Then how soon may I come?'

'The room is ready. You may as well stay. I will send Felix down to fetch your baggage and he can explain matters and pay your bill.'

'Why, you have smoothed away all my difficulties!'

'You cannot stay among those people! Merienda will be ready in ten minutes. Socorro will bring you towels. You empty the water so – You see?'

'Yes. I see. Thank you for allowing me to come to your house, señora.'

'Do you think you will be staying all the summer? For the season?'

'If you will allow me,' I replied, smiling as I spoke, though she deliberately withdrew before my obvious advance of friendliness.

'We are all Christians under this roof you understand me?'

'I am not a Catholic,' I explained.

'That is because you know no better, I am sure,' she said finally. 'At any rate, you are English – and the English are always proper,' I felt I was taking unfair advantage of her ignorance, but did not say so.

'We shall be alone in the house for some weeks. I expect you will find it dull.'

'I am sure I shall be very happy'.

'Ah! You are very young to be so sure of that! '

'SSeññorrra!' bawled a female voice. 'There is a lack of sugar!'

'What stupidity is this! I gave it out this morning!'

'No, SSEÑÑORRRA! This morning there was the caramel custard to prepare for the priests' luncheon party to-morrow and – Oh, Pardon! Pardon!' Socorro, the waiting maid, stood agape in the doorway.

'What stupidity! Go to the kitchen at once! I am coming.'

I thought Teresa spoke with unnecessary severity. But I soon learned that Socorro was not very quick of understanding. She was a typical Asturian country-lass, tall, loose-limbed, always agape at everything everybody did or said. Ungainly now at the age of twenty, she was made to bear and carry children through the length of her days. She had an engaging look of simplicity, though, large grey eyes, and a mass of dull, fair hair which straggled down either side over the front of her shoulders. She had a way of bursting into laughter when you spoke to her and picked at the folds of her apron when replying

to questions. Had she been able to read, Socorro would have senti-
mentalised over life and sighed much more than she smiled. As it was,
she laughed at everything; all the more because she did not know why
she did so.

Felix was well named, and as neat and nimble as a sailor; always
helpful and willing; so far as I could see, decorous to every woman,
and affable in an unassuming, quiet way. He was handsome, too;
grey-eyed and fair like Socorro, though with crisp, curled hair, and
with an alert, innocently lively expression of curiosity which Teresa's
severity could never wholly quell. Though in her presence the rising
sap in her younger dependents appeared dormant, it mounted again
as soon as she was out of sight. But in spite of her warning shadow
of oppression, even the ancient Tio Francisco, who had served in the
second Carlist War, had moments of irrepressible chuckling and cack-
ling when the sun warmed his bones or particularly appetising odours
wreathed up from the kitchen. At such times he would urge the
canary to fresh flourishes of whistling with uncouth snappings of his
fingers accompanied by rather horrid gobbling sounds in his throat.
Only Teresa's threats to have the canary sent 'beyond the mountains'
could cow him.

I had not been in the house a day before Felix confided in me while
watching me eat the dishes he served that he had a great longing to
go to England. I was surprised and said so.

'Why, you seem so thoroughly contented and cheerful where you
are.'

'Ah, señorita! But one can earn money there, they say. Money!'

'And why do you want money?' I enquired. 'What is your ambition?'

'I want to buy a bicycle,' was his simple reply.

'That is a modest wish, I should think,' said I, glad he was not
more mercenary

'Could I earn sufficient money in England to buy a bicycle, señorita?'

'Why, yes. It should not take very long to do that. Surely here, too?'

'No, no señorita. Not here.' However much I rub and polish up the
gold and silver in the sacristy of San Roque and sweep and wash the
floors, though I should clean the chapel for ever I shall never earn
enough to get that bicycle here. Never, never, señorita!'

'You seem very anxious to get that bicycle. Do you want to become
Champion in the Grand National Tour of Spain, Felix?'

'Ah, no, not for that! You see the grave of my father and mother and my little brother, too, is thirty miles away. As things are, I cannot get to tend it – already it is growing to look neglected and there is no one else. Now, if I had a bicycle I could go over every month on my free day. My little brother – well, señorita, he was my little brother – and my father and mother, well, they were my mother and father, of course!' Here Felix unaccountably burst out laughing and looked not in the least sad about it at all, but Teresa appeared in the doorway, whereupon he was thoughtful at once.

'Felix' she thundered in harsh warning.

'Coming! Coming!' and he withdrew to bring my coffee while I leisurely peeled Canary bananas and early Santander peaches, small, green and hard.

Pine-trees peered down on the windows of the long, tiled room in which I ate. Down to the right, one could catch glimpses of the Cantabrian sea, still grey and yellow and foaming white with the storms of late spring. The walls were tiled with a clear, defined pattern of terracotta, green and black, and there was a provincial, ornate hand-basin to the right of the door, outlined in porcelain blue and yellow traceries. But it was an empty, mocking room. Felix told me that I had come much, much too early, before the lobster and ice-cream vendors found it worthwhile to trundle up their wares from the town. 'In a month we may have a sprinkling, chiefly those shy creatures who fear their fellow men and only leave their family retreats inland one month in the year. Later we shall be half full and after that – Psst! I shall be slung out to sleep under those pines, señorita, while the King's secretaries play poker with each other for my room. They always arrive last with their portfolios, poor fellows, when the Palace is full.'

'We shall all be very grand, no doubt, and have to mind our behaviour.'

'No doubt! The King's great-aunt, you know, has the Sanctuary under her personal and very royal protection. A few more charitable ladies like her and there would be no more talk of revolution. Pssst! They say our fish and the milk and butter are the finest in all Spain and that you can dine off our streets, we keep them so spotless. They say we are very clean, here. I hope the señorita finds us clean?'

'Truly, yes!' I had finished my coffee.

'Well, I must set the tables for our reverend betters. They will be here within an hour.'

'Felix!' called Teresa, as though she was uttering an imprecation.

'All is ready, señora,' he called back, reassuringly.

'For twelve, to-day, Felix'.

'Yes, señora! For the twelve apostles I am ready, if need be! ' His manner was so disarming, his wit so artless and his speech so politely deferring that one could never take offence. I got up to go.

'It is a kind of conclave this afternoon, señorita, to make arrangements for the Festival of San Roque; two or three padres come up from the town, some others from over the hills at Comillas.'

'Ah, Comillas! I should like to visit the Seminary some day'.

'Why not? Don Luis could invite you. Well, I must see to the wines. It is quite a sight, believe me, señorita, when we of San Roque entertain the world, spiritual or otherwise. But that is seldom, naturally. It is no light responsibility, the charge of our Sanctuary, señorita. But doña Teresa is equal to any man, everyone agrees. She misses nothing, nothing! Psst!' Teresa showed the truth of this by calling him again and I left the sala and retired to my room.

I did not see the party, but I heard it. Late luncheon, begun at something to three o'clock, merged into merienda at something past six before the Fathers and Brothers trooped and shuffled out in solid jocularity and assembled themselves upon the balcony. Outside, there leaned in the gutter a dingy, dusty, dilapidated, battered and bespattered Austin Seven. I had never seen a car so much the worse for wear and so little the better for all the spirituality of its many owners. I soon saw the reason why. Of the twelve priests, seven proposed to ride in it all the way on the long, mountainous track to Comillas. Four reverend, black-robed fathers, the largest, made a simultaneous charge upon the little car. Two got in by force of battering, head and beaver hats downwards, ahead of the others. The third, of less authority but more adroit, quickly squeezed himself into the space by the driver. Then two others, large men, too, attempted an assault, both on the back seats. Now, had the priests been moderately lean something might have been done, but they were all persons of obvious authority, as firmly and fully determined of will as they were firm and full of flesh. There were two juniors only, and these, by no mere coincidence, had the shriven aspect of underlings, and dare not mount until their superiors were settled. The two priests could not get in – but then, much worse predicament, they could not get out again. Their discomfort was evident and exquisite. They all rose, perforce, and the car lurched, rocked, heaved, rose, swayed, bounced, and nearly turned turtle with its wrestling load of overbearing cargo. Only the driver, who was putting on gloves in the gateway, and the priests from the town, who shared the duties of San Roque, stood talking unconcerned, though not unamused at all the pother and not unaware of the smothered signs of distress and sounds of alarm, discreetly suppressed.

All had to begin again, except the adroit father in front, who sat still and gazed firmly on the distance, determined not to become involved in the mounting battle again. With side-about squeezings they angled for corners and were pinned down mercilessly by the oncoming remainder for their pains. The sallow, liverish-looking neophytes sidled up with deprecating gestures and looked towards the driver for instructions. 'One at each side' he ordered. 'One must stand.' 'Both must stand! Both must stand!' cried those already mounted.

Ay! Ay! Ay! came forth winces and muttered wails, as the priestlings trod upon the toes of their superiors. Shoulders were raised, apologies tendered and scarcely accepted. The driver approached the off-side of the car. Once more it heaved and lurched as he squeezed himself in and banged the door.

'But where is Luis? Where is Luis?' cried the chief among them.

'Doña Teresa, where is your nephew? Where is Luis?'

'Really, this grows more difficult every time,' murmured the first. 'Look for him in the dining-room. He was still there when we came out. Where is doña Teresa? Really! We shall be late for supper.'

'Luis, Luis!' called Teresa in the doorway. 'He is coming now!' Testy looks were turned upon Luis as he stumblingly descended, wiping his mouth, chin and vestments with one hand, while with the other he hastily stuffed something into the placket pocket of his pleated skirts. He was a closely-cropped, square-headed young priest, with a stupid, obstinate air and the jog-trot walk of a peasant. He looked at the loaded vehicle and halted.

'It is not possible. It is not possible', murmured the fathers.

'You came thus,' retorted the priest of San Roque, not very kindly. 'He will have to stand in front. There is no other way'.

'Not on my brakes,' said the driver politely but with the finality of the knowing mechanic who is the god of his machine, among a tribe of unenlightened infidels.

'You know those bends and the gradient!'

Yes, they evidently remembered both the bends and the gradient.

'I cannot imagine why we have this trouble every time, every time!', said the chief among them, trying to convey an atmosphere of benign resignation. 'After all, what is the use of making a car to take seven if it cannot take eight at a pinch?'

'It is the horsepower, señor, not the seating capacity! I have tried to explain that to you before', said the mechanic.

'It has nothing whatever to do with horses. How can it? Do get it started, if you please.' The tone was less benign, more authoritarian. The driver seemed to think it better not to attempt an argument, so he took it out of the car which shook convulsively under his diabolical rape. In desperation, Luis hurled himself upon the priest in front who threw him off in a most unchristian frenzy of self-defence. There was a clatter and roar. Heads were bent low, beaver hats clutched tightly and in a slowly rising swathe of dust the extenuated Austin coughed out of sight.

'Now, if they had had bicycles' murmured Felix, coming up the steps. 'Don Luis has left his pastries behind! See, señora!' Felix held up a pyramidical packet by its loop of string. 'How disconsolate he will be now. Ay! They should have sent him to a nunnery.'

'They will serve for the señorita's tea,' ordered Teresa. 'It is already very late.'

'It doesn't matter now', I said. 'I will wait till dinner'.

'Ah! no!' responded Felix, shaking his head at my ignorance. 'Dinner will be late in proportion – or later. I will bring your tea immediately.'

'Then I will have it in the dining-room to save time, shall I?'

The sight in the dining-room was memorable. Comparison with the fragments left over from the feeding of the five thousand instantly rose to one's mind. The floor was like an English heath after a Londoners' bank holiday. Silver paper, bits of biscuits, crusts of sodden bread, orange and miscellaneous fruit peelings, banana skins, torn paper napkins exuding tomato pulp and salad shreds, sweetmeat twists, spilled coffee cups, crumbs, crumbs everywhere. It might have been the leavings of a charabanc load. But no! It was only a sign that an ecclesiastical collation had been enjoyed. I could not help it. I sat down at the piano and sang the eighteenth century song, a Madrid burlesque upon the appetite of priests.

'Por colación seis abates	'For a collation six priests
Se comieron un canario	Sat down to feast on a canary
Y aun dejaron a cenar	And even left over sufficient
Para la estatua del Prado	For the supper of the statue in
	the Prado!'

Felix leaned on the table and laughed and shook his head.

'But not Don Francisco's canary! Not Don Francisco's canary, señorita, please! ' I became aware of a grim silence behind the frosted glass window.

Then Socorro appeared and began to help Felix clear away the tables.

'The sseññora is very annoyed with you for speaking so of Don Luis.' She whispered.

'Pssst! Why should she? He is not her nephew. His status is no more than that of Anibal, who was adopted by her brother and bequeathed to doña Teresa by will. The good opinion of Anibal is much more difficult to obtain, I assure you, and that is what counts! You cannot win Anibal's good favour with a few *pasteles*. Besides, what is wrong with a nunnery?'

On the next day I set off at about three o'clock to wander over the lower foothills of the Asturian mountain range to the north-west. I was in search for clues to problems of musical study which no books or lectures could solve. When I left the Villa the sky was a pearly mist. I had not realised how soon such skies broke down into persistent rain in these parts. But in spite of this, the vegetation on this side was rank and sparse and it seemed that only a bare subsistence was to be scratched from the soil. I went up and on; present day living conditions were soon left behind, and even the rude stone-piled huts were scarce. The only sign of truck with modern ways was the single electric cable exposed from one pole to another up the mountain sides. So remote and untrodden were these parts that when I approached any cabins or hovels children ran before me howling and screaming with fear at the appearance of a stranger. In spite of the rain and the forbidding looks of things I wandered on till I was satisfied that the difference between the melodies of this area and those of its neighbouring valleys could be ascribed to the bleakness of Nature and not to the survival of a 'pocket' of some as yet unidentified primitive race of a type like the Basques, many miles away to the east. Well! Let them evolve their ingenious little theories and lecture and write against one another in the great capitals and universities of the world. I was satisfied with my own solution and cheerfully submitted to a thorough wetting. All the same, the downpour was developing into a storm, so, thinking of finding a short cut back to San Roque, I turned sharply southeast. After all, it was a sanctuary of more than local fame and surely one or other of these downward plunging tracks should lead in its direction.

But then the mist descended heavily and I found myself climbing again in spite of my efforts to go downhill. I turned about and found another track, but again I found myself climbing. There was a rumble of thunder now. The solving of musical problems on one's own seemed a piece of absurdly youthful folly. I was lost.

Suddenly there came up to me an uncouth noise, as of sheep or goats scrambling and shambling on a cliff s edge. I made towards it and all at once found myself confronted by the most outlandish figure I had ever seen. Breached to the knee, but bare-legged below, cowled and hooded on his back with a sulphur-dyed goatskin, a weird man stood in my path brandishing a thick club. His face was nearly covered with a thick white stubble and tufts of blackish hair sprouted out of his nostrils. I was frightened and shrank back. He gesticulated and mumbled. He had few teeth in his head, but I did not like the hungry look in his eyes. You are more wolf than man, I said to myself in dismay. I tried to turn aside off the track but again he barred my way down. But he did not attempt to touch me. It was impossible to make out what he was saying until I realised that he was pointing all the time to a rift in the cliff, bidding me take shelter. I did not like the idea at all. How did I know what others of his kind were in that cave? But there was a nearer rumble, then the crash of boulders from somewhere above and a clatter down the mountain. And again the rain lashed at us. Nature or man, which could I trust? So, unwillingly, I made signs that I would follow him and away he leaped before me, twirling his club. But at the entrance to the cave I stopped. My courage failed me. Then, all at once, the mist lifted and the sun drifted waterily through the clouds. I saw myself standing on the edge of a great precipice of smooth dark rock, more than half way up the face of a mountain isolated from the Asturian range whose foothills I had set out to explore. I turned about at once, looking for a gleam of the sea that would show me where home and San Roque lay.

I suppose I started to move, for suddenly a hand was laid on my arm, and a woman's voice said imploringly; 'Señorita! Señorita!' I turned round to the mouth of the cave again. Before me stood a woe-begone creature, with a pleading, pitiful look on her face.

'Please to enter! Please to enter!' she begged. I could not ignore such an earnest appeal, so, wondering what awaited me, I stepped into the darkness behind her. Immediately I was breathing that strange atmosphere, commingled damp and heat, of the innermost entrañas of the earth. For a few moments I could make out nothing at all except the crags which lowered around us and forbade the further penetration of any creature larger than a goat. Then I perceived a little lamp lit and before me on the ground a muddled heap of rags and clothing moving faintly up and down.

'Señorita!' implored the woman, drawing me nearer to that heap. She bent down and drew back the coverings. There lay three young children, unconscious, in the last stages, it seemed, of some terrifying fever. Their tongues lolled against their lips and their throats were swollen and gave forth a sickening smell that made me uneasy in my soul. I drew back and looked at the woman.

'Three days!' she said. 'Three days!'

'But – a doctor?' I questioned. The woman shrugged her shoulders. She looked at the crucifix above the little lamp.

'You must get a doctor,' I urged.

'No money', the man said. 'No money. What doctor would come so far?'

'I will go back and see what can be done. They must be taken to a hospital.'

'Look, Señorita, look! They are like dead already. No hospital would take them.

'Cover them up again. I will fetch help immediately.' The man looked unbelieving. 'Here! Take this in the meantime.' I gave her two duro pieces of silver. 'Look! the rain has stopped. I will send help, I promise you. Only point out my quickest way back to San Roque. I am staying in the house by the sanctuary.'

'Well! Gracias! Gracias! The priest may come, perhaps, when you tell him they are dying.'

'I know nothing or very little about the priests, but I will find a doctor.' They still seemed incredulous, though grateful for the money. The man led me outside and round the bend towards a slippery gully. There he left me; the way was plain enough in the clear evening light.

Half in tears, for the fright I had had and the plight of the family in the reeking, gloomy cave, I stumbled over the loose rocks and jagged stones down the gully which I guessed to be the occasional bed of a spring mountain torrent in times of flood, and made all haste I could. In not much more than an hour I was within sight of San Roque and, wet and distracted, I flew up the stone steps of the Villa Heliotrope.

'She is back! She is back!' cried Felix, darting in with the news.

Teresa met me in he doorway. 'What is this?' she began sternly. 'If this is what it means to go searching for lost music …! '

'I was setting out in search of you,' said Felix. We were anxious.' I began to tremble and shiver, I could not tell why.

'Of course you are wet through and have caught a chill if not worse!' Teresa confronted me accusingly.

'No, no, not I. It is for them – a doctor. I must get a doctor at once, at once.' They all stood and stared at me, even Tio Francisco stole out from his rush chair under the canary's cage to have a look at me. The tears streamed down my face, but somehow I stammered out my tale. It was one thing to make myself clear in my limited Spanish in calm moments of ordinary affairs; but in time of stress the words would not come. Teresa took me by the arm, for by now I was shaking from head to foot, and made me sit down in a high-backed chair while she looked at me attentively, but without comment. I re-told my tale.

'Tio!' she called. 'Go down and see if Father Ignacio can come at once.'

When the priest arrived I was drinking an infusion of herbs. Teresa herself had drawn off my wet shoes and stockings and muffled my feet and legs in a rough towel. Socorro came and went with pans of scalding water, agape as usual and gasping 'Ay! Jesús! Ay! Jesús! Qué señorita!'

Teresa and Father Ignacio had a quick dialogue, too rapid for me to understand. Then they seemed at a standstill till Felix joined in.

'She means the Peña de Vieja Castilla. I know the gully.'

'Ah! That is the parish of Santo Antonio.'

'Si, Si,' said Felix. 'Santo Antonio it is!'

'You have been there alone!' exclaimed Teresa. 'Excuse me, Father!' she turned to him with an exculpating gesture.

'Well, we will see what can be done.'

'A doctor! I assure you, a doctor must be sent!' I continued to urge.

'Father Ignacio will do what is proper,' said Teresa.

'And they must be got away from that place. You cannot leave fellow human beings in such a dreadful plight!'

Father Ignacio got up very abruptly and went to the door. Teresa followed him, exchanged a few more words, then he went away and she came back.

'You must go to bed at once,' she said curtly.

'Oh, I am all right, thank you. It is the shock.'

'What shock?'

'Those unhappy, destitute people, living like animals, abandoned, in misery – in a cave! '

'But why should they not live in a cave?'

I looked up with astonishment. I gaped as wide as Socorro now.

'But – in a cave – one's fellow creatures ...

'Are there no caves in England, then?'

'Yes, but nobody lives in them! Why, it would not be allowed!'

'Is that your freedom then?' I looked at her quickly. I had seen the corners of her mouth lift ever so slightly.

'Here there are many who live in the caves, whole communities, who count themselves very lucky, I can tell you.'

'Lucky!' I echoed her. And now she smiled for the first time since I had met her.

'Yes, indeed! Why, think of it! They pay no rent, no tithes, no taxes. The police leave them alone, as a rule. There are no holes in the roof for the rain to come in; the floors are sound; the walls are thick and the wind never penetrates.'

'Yes, but those children are dying!'

'My child, children are dying everywhere. Do you not know it? Born and bred up there, who can say what they have escaped hitherto? They are their own masters, those people. And that is something. That is a very great deal, if you ask me! ' She sounded a grimmer note here. 'And now,' she said resuming her brisk household manner. 'And now you will go to bed. And you shall have lentil soup and no sweet for the fright you have given us all this evening! Socorro! Is that copper pan filled yet for the señorita's bed?' And so I betook myself to my room.

Later, Teresa came in to see how I was. I was wide awake.

'Well!' she surveyed me. 'You did not find what you were looking for today?

'I was not looking for anything in particular.'

'Not even for some of those pretty songs? The lost pretty songs that haunt your ears, as you say?'

'No, señora. I never look for them. They never come to order, in that way. One trusts to luck and then they come without bidding, or, as one of your dramatists says, one learns to expect nothing and then some day the miracle arrives.

'Ah, I see ... You, too, trust in some divine accident, even for your lost songs. Is that it?'

'Señora, do you think there is any hope for those children?'

'Why not? Perhaps you are a divine accident in their lives! Had you thought of that?' I could not tell whether she was teasing or not: it was not like her to tease.

'No, no! I hadn't,' was all I ventured to say. Thereupon she laughed. It was gone in a moment, but at the sound I sat bolt upright in bed. For it was like an elf in merriment in a forest, standing alone and watching a human being's attempt to find its way out. I always trusted to my ears without question. Somewhere, beneath all that impersonality and harshness, there was still a flicker of youth in Teresa. And suddenly I longed to fan it alight.

Then Socorro called bleatingly along the corridor. 'Sseññorra! Sseññorra!'

'What is it? What is it? Not so much noise. I am coming! ' Once more her voice was hard and grating, as if a stiff key were turning in a stubborn lock.

But after that evening I fancied that though she kept a private door in her mind fast closed against all else, yet it would move ajar at a slight push from me. I could not tell why. On the next day Felix informed me that in future dinner would be laid for me in her own private room; the comedor was too draughty in this changeable weather and it was too empty to be pleasant, he explained. So that same evening I made my way into the dark little room on the right and there under a low hanging lamp I ate, alone, in a less vasty atmosphere, though cheerless still. Tio Francisco supped a bowl of sops in the kitchen by the stove. Teresa never sat down with me to eat, of course, but gradually she came in and out, covertly watching my plate and my appetite, and whether I enjoyed one dish more than another. When I could make out the details, I discovered that the solid, large cupboard which filled up all one wall of the room opposite the door was a double confessional box. All the priestly mending to be done was kept locked up here and only taken out to be aired, examined and repaired under her strict supervision. Some of the vestments were richly sewn and embroidered, these were the feast-day accoutrements of the diocese, and even the ordinary stoles and surplices had borders of fine lace-work. A bunch of artificial flowers under a glass case stood before a faded image of the Virgin. There was the low table, a few solidly carved rush-bottomed chairs and little else.

Unexpected delicacies began to appear on my trays: sugared sponge-fingers with my morning chocolate as well as the rolls and butter with quince preserve; then there were saffron-flavoured and honey-cream pastries for merienda, with such occasional luxuries as candied cherries and sweet-coated nuts.

I discovered that Tio Francisco was despatched down to the town three times a week for these, wet or fine. He always wore the peaked cap of his old militia regiment indoors and out, and when he went down to the town he enveloped his lean frame in the ancient gabardine cloak which had once completed his uniform of the far-off Carlist campaigns. He was a forceful walker for his age – he was upwards of eighty – and had the stealthy catlike tread of a man from the hills. On the days he was not sent down to the town he roamed the more grassy slopes inland in search of one or two peculiar kinds of flowering grasses to which the canary was partial. Then he would march into the house waving his posies with infantile glee: 'For the canario! For the canario!' he would chuckle, and at sight of the grasses the canary would flutter from perch to perch, chirping for pleasure. Tio Francisco had the bluest eyes I ever saw in a Spaniard; very light they were and opaque. Age had brought his beaky nose and bony chin very close together and I could not be sure whether the pinched, rather mean expression he wore when not engaged in colloquy with the canario was due to the falling-in of the facial structure or whether behind the apparent innocence of the blue eyes had once worked a calculating self-interested brain. But whatever character he had once possessed was now almost entirely blotted out in the mist of senility. Only one other habit of his persisted in my memory. When he was dozing beneath the canary's cage and the house was quiet his long bony fingers would make strange passes in the air, fretting and plucking as if to disentangle his dreams from some invisible cob-web that threatened to envelop them. These queer gestures puzzled me and persisted in disturbing some unthinking corner of my brain.

Teresa, however, did not approve of my attempts to make his better acquaintance, so I soon gave up all thought of it. I was allowed to infer that Tio Francisco had had a flighty youth and a murky maturity and that it was a lucky day for him when he found his last asylum in her house. I made much allowance for Teresa's strait outlook on life; but though it was plain that whatever mischief he had been capable of had long since shrivelled up within him, still she seemed to think that some breath of contamination might yet infect the air unless he were segregated. In the company of his beloved canary he seemed the final essence of purity; perhaps this was an instance of that last triumph of innocence over experience. The primitive colours combined of the yellow canary, Tio Francisco's blue eyes and red and pink apple cheeks added to this suggestion of childlike blamelessness.

Compared to this conventional picture, the darkness of Teresa's hue and dresses – always black – against the streaked gaudiness of the parrot, the harsh rigours of their unwordy exchanges, suggested a far-fetched extravaganza. As the old Portuguese ballad says, the precise years of a woman's age are of no consequence; what matters is that she should display a desire to please (the singer is, of course, a man). Teresa was not old; but she certainly displayed no wish to please or charm, any more than Anibal sought to entice strange passions. She did not love the parrot, nor did the parrot love her. Yet there was a mutual pact between them, more firm than many emotional attachments. Whatever else the morning's tasks required, there were always ten minutes or more put aside for Anibal's ritual shower bath on the balcony in the hot climbing sun. She herself would bring his perch out of the kitchen and Felix would fetch the watering-can with the sprinkler. Before the show began, Anibal would blink in the strong light after the dimness of the kitchen and move nervously up and down his perch. But when she lifted up the watering-can he would lift up his wing-feathers and squawk a greeting to the world. Then down would patter the drops in an iridescent shower and he would tremble with voluptuous pleasure. The watering done, Teresa would put her forefinger within reach of his beak for him to nip and nip again. Then he would squawk once more and address any passers-by with ribald low phrases. Then he liked her to scratch softly the queer carbuncle that protruded above his left eye, after which he steamed and basked above the heliotrope till lunch. This carbuncle gave him the cross-eyed, sinister look of one who has had nefarious traffic with the underworld. It was probably the consequence of considerable age, but no one had any idea of the real length of his days. There was a tradition that he had come originally from Pernambuco, though obviously his speech had been acquired elsewhere. But whatever the thoughts of past times he brooded upon during the long silences in his kitchen lair, to us they remained as dark and mysterious and impenetrable as the Amazonian jungle.

Teresa had had a half-brother, considerably older than herself, who was an officer in the Spanish navy. He had brought her the parrot after a long cruise in American waters, almost his last voyage before the Cuban war in which he lost his life, so that Anibal became a last bequest which, as Felix affirmed, she never repudiated, in spite of the offence its bastard language had given on occasion to the more academically-minded among her summer visitors. It seemed more than coincidence that Anibal reserved his most disgraceful remarks exclusively to mock at these fastidious guests and argued against the theory of the merely mechanical repetitiveness of the parrot tribe.

Her half-brother had left his family another legacy in Luis, son of his servant, a naval rating killed only a little while before him, with instructions that one half of his pension should be put aside towards the boy's education, for the priesthood, if possible. This bequest she had also dutifully fulfilled, though again there was little emotion in the relationship between them. Luis was ungainly and stupid, but somehow he had stayed the course of training which he was expected to conclude this summer. No one knew what was to be done with Luis then, said Felix, who was my informant on most matters. Teresa abstained from all comment on him.

Against my better judgement the piano had been set up in the dining-room. My wish to have it in my own room was attributed to excess of modesty, and I gave up trying to explain that the tiled walls of the long room would produce deafening reverberations from the piano's iron frame. The kitchen lay along one side of the dining-room and I wondered how Anibal would behave when I began my first morning's exercises. All seemed to prosper at first. He made no sound, and I began to think myself secure in his acquiescence. Alas! I was mistaken. I was permitted with no protest from him to vocalise scales, common chords and arpeggios even to the seventh degree of the dominant. But then, inevitably, I reached the singer's climax of virtuosity – the trill. Steadily I made my way up, trilling on *Mi* and *Fa*. On *Sol* I heard a flutter of wings and a raucous clearing of a most unbirdlike throat. On *La* Anibal took up the tale and I was submerged. Something roused in him the ungodly spirit of emulation. Trill he would and trill he should. It was ridiculous, ludicrous, it was frightful. I know nothing of the normal extension of a parrot's voice, but at least it was obvious that Anibal was not vocally made for high acrobatics. But alas! I had presented him with a new idea, another goal for life, and from note to note he swung uncertainly like a drunken booby clinging aloft at dizzying height to the unfamiliar trapeze ropes upon which he has been thrown in a frolic and totally unable to descend. I soon stopped; then din was indescribable. But nothing would stop him. The whole kitchen was in an uproar. Trays were banged about his head, tin lids and saucepans clashed and clattered. Socorro, threw her apron over her head and threatened to add a bout of hysterics to the pandemonium.

But still Anibal warbled on and up, always striving for that trill on La, becoming frenzied to a pitch of self-strangulation. Ambition is a fiery steed when once he has you mounted. So thought Felix, who advanced upon Anibal with a bucket of water intending to put him out and quench the fever that enraged him. But Teresa would not have this and there began a rousing argument which added to the din. Then she snatched up Tio Francisco's dark gabardine cloak and flung it over the now contorted bird. From underneath he struggled on with fitful squawks and shrieks, till gasping for breath he succumbed to an unnatural exhaustion and was carried out to take the air, glazed of eye and apoplectically convulsing.

We gazed at one another speechless. What then? Having caught our affectations of speech, was it possible a bird might take infection from our passions also? Away in the distance, the little canary was serenely descanting, fluting his *obbligato* to a melody from some other sphere wherein ambition had no place. He seemed to suggest an answer to my question, but what it was I could not catch.

'You must not be discouraged,' said Felix to me at lunch. 'It was the – you know –' here he wagged two fingers backwards and forwards suggestively, starting slowly and getting quicker and quicker.

'Yes, yes, I know. The trill,' I said shortly. I did not want to discuss the affair.

'Yes, señorita, the – what you said, exactly! Anibal did not mind the rest. Really, believe me, he did not mind it all. You must not be discouraged. Try again tomorrow, señorita. He will get used to it in time. Try again to-morrow.'

'Thank you. I will try not to be discouraged, as you say. But to-morrow is Sunday so we will call a truce.'

'Yes, señorita. Believe me, it is as I say. It was the –' and he waggled his fingers again – 'what you said. The señorita understands that break-fast will of course be late to-morrow because everyone gets up so early?'

Felix was irrepressible.

I leaned over my bedroom window-sill a long time that night. The warmer weather from the south was creeping up under cover of heavy thunder-clouds and frequent storms of rain. To-night the light-ning played about the margin of the clouds more vividly than I had ever seen before and it made magnificent sword-play far across the horizon as if threatening an unnatural dawn. Perhaps that was why the cocks began crowing soon after midnight and kept calling and challenging one another all over the mountainsides. I wondered whether Teresa was asleep. Then to my surprise I found myself won-dering whether she prayed at night. I could not remember that I had ever had such a thought about anyone before, certainly not in England. Here, of course, it was different. One could not escape the subject. It pressed on life all around.

I sensed some deep disturbance in her life. The constraint she put upon herself was quite violent; it was that which made her so harsh of speech and threw such dark shadows before and behind her pres-ence. Yet there was that sudden, shrill little laugh of amusement. I liked the recollection of that sound enormously. Yet why should I bother myself? Teresa evidently kept herself to herself and had her reasons for doing so. Quite right! To steer my own course was as much as I could manage. Teresa after all, had found an anchorage of sorts, but where was mine to be? One went on from day to day, in moderately calm weather, drifting scarcely at all, but if a gale blew up and carried me out to the open sea, what then? I was not even sure that my own little boat was water-tight.

Teresa, I suddenly realised, was well battened down. She was tak-ing no chances. That argued that she had weathered considerable storms in her time. Well! At least I had assured her of my sympathy, though not in words.

Some heavy drops of rain were falling now, so I withdrew my elbows from the window-sill and went to bed, though not to sleep. I turned my pillow and found the subject turning also.

Unlike everyone else, Teresa alone showed no sign of deferring to the growing heat. She alone had never shivered in the damp spring mists nor crossed herself during any storm. So now I never heard her complain of the sun, nor use a fan with a half-impatient 'Ay! Jesús!' like the rest of womankind. But then she seldom went out of doors except for the morning ceremonial bathing of Anibal. Once or twice of an evening, however, when I sat alone on the balcony breathing in the scent of the expanding heliotrope, now climbing boldly over the stone curved pillars, she would come and stand behind me in the doorway for a few moments, then go away for a while, and come again, to stand quite motionless, more like a shadow to my thoughts than a companion.

She grew even more attentive to my personal tastes and distastes, however. But it was warily done, as though she were trying to deny that these demonstrations of interest in me were of a private kind; and when I tried politely to disguise my lack of enthusiasm for some of her local dishes, it was as if we were playing a game of pretence for some stake of human emotion whose potentiality we tacitly agreed to ignore. I did not like saffron in any dish, sweet or savoury; it vanished. I did not like cinnamon. That absented itself, except as an adornment to egg-rice pudding. I did not like goats-flesh, nor kid, even. Certainly I could not stomach conger-eel. These disappeared, though never a word passed between us on the subject. I found her delicacy of observation quite exceptional, for Spanish women rarely show much discrimination either in their own tastes or in considering the tastes of others. For some reason or other, Teresa liked to have me there; though she made no sign, I felt the approach of a more explicit acknowledgement in the air between us. I went on collecting my songs, comparing and arranging them, singing and playing. The canary whistled, Tio Francisco chirruped and chucked with it, the parrot squawked uneasily in his siesta doze, or screamed to the occasional passer-by who loitered in the way, Felix joked incessantly and Socorro gaped her exclamations of wonder at everything in life that came her way, perhaps because that was so little, for our only visitor from the town was doña Clara, a pallid rich and pious widow, who was constantly alarming her nephews and nieces – her nephews particularly – by the fertility with which she invented new ways of charitably expending her late husband's not inconsiderable fortune. This spring it had occurred to her to repeat up at the Sanctuary the latest electrical installation of multi-coloured altar illumination which she had provided for one of the dockland church-es. But she was still undecided whether to spend her dividends up here or to install an electrical organ in another of the town churches, also with coloured beams of light, which, she explained, she had seen the autumn before when on a visit to Barcelona, where one had been inau-gurated in the latest cinema. She came and went regularly once a week, discussing the problem as she and Teresa examined the altar cloths and vestments or cut out clothing for the girls of the local remand-home to sew for their babies.

But one night after doña Clara had gone, Teresa came out and sat herself down beside me.

'It is very dull for you up here,' she began. 'Well, the children will be here soon, and you will not be so lonely then.'

'But I am not lonely now.'

'But of course you are. I thought you would have gone long ago.'

'When you have taken care to look after me so well?'

'I? I have done nothing at all. Nothing at all.'

'Well, here I am still and of my own free will, you see.'

'Yes – you have your own free will, as you call it.'

'You speak enviously, it seems.'

'Not for myself – but perhaps for the girl I once was.' She stopped so abruptly that the pause served to underline her words.

'Don't you realise' I said after a pause 'that this travelling about from place to place in the English way, and American too, now, is a sign of weakness, of essential nothingness, a postponing of – of ...'

'A postponing of what?' But I did not stay to answer that.

'Why, it is you Spaniards who live in one spot, close to your roots, who have a strength and continuity, a force of concentration which dis-concerts the wanderer who feels himself disintegrating and crumbling before your certainty of relationship to the place in which you live?'

'Strength from our roots! Do you mean our chains?'

'Doña Teresa, here we are talking like the men-folk, generalising, abstracting ...! When we have more interesting things to tell each other. You came here from over the mountains, did you not?'

'Oh yes, but that was long ago, as measured by your life, Nanita.'

'But not so far as all that.'

'No, not so far, perhaps. Yet ...' she looked out across the hills – 'yet – not so far, nor so long ago, neither. Sometimes it is rather like when on a clear day after rain you see into the mountain ranges and Reina Clara seems almost within sight then, though it is a day's journey by train, a very tiring, troublesome day, too, not worth the aggravations.

'In many ways your life here is probably more pleasant?'

'What makes you think so? It is different, that is all.'

'Have you relatives there still?'

'No. They are all gone. Except, of course, a second cousin and those, of course – but they have forgotten me by now.'

'I suppose among the mountains Reina Clara is shut in for a good many months of the year?'

'One is always shut in there.'

'Are there wolves there still, for instance?'

'Oh yes. In bad times they come right down into the streets at night and everything is barred and barricaded.'

'And did you ever see one, doña Teresa? I mean, prowling about?'

'I remember as a child getting up in the morning and being shown their footmarks in the snow.

'And did you hear them howling?'

She smiled briefly at my ignorance. 'The wolves come silently when they come to town.'

'And bears?'

'Bears! We had one stuffed to stand at the door for a boot-scraper. My grandfather was a great huntsman in the mountains. But as I say, it is fifteen years since I left all that.'

'You have no family left, then?'

'I left Reina Clara when my mother died. Soon after.' She said this very curtly.

'Had you friends here, at that time, that you chose San Roque?'

'No. It was arranged. My mother's great-uncle had been Bishop of the province – long ago, naturally, – and so – with the money – and knowing I wished to go away, it was all arranged.'

'Your character must have been well known there.'

'What do you say?' she frowned at me harshly.

'Why, your administrative gifts, your organising ability. They are evident in everything you do.'

'Oh – that! ' She shrugged her little shoulders, in disdain of herself.

'Why do you despise it? Think how most women's lives grow narrower and narrower as they grow older – and how your activities expand!'

'That is nothing. Nothing! Believe me!'

'Many women would envy you your powers.'

'Powers for what, pray?'

'Why, powers to do what you wish.'

'I? The power to do what I wish? Do you think I ever had that?'

'You have it now.'

'When I have ceased to wish? When there is nothing left of life for me to wish for! ' She drew her black shawl tightly across her breasts.

'That seems to be when power comes to us, if we are lucky enough to be born wiser than our blood.' I said, barely conscious of my own words.

'To be born wiser than our blood! And who wants that?' There was a rising note of impatience in her voice now.

'None of us, I suspect,' I agreed with her.

'The only power I ever felt in me was not my own – never my own – but from those other things that blow through us and lift us up and whirl us about so that we don't know what we are doing, or why, or whether we are willing or not. NO! Power of any sort I never wished to have. I have seen only too well what it does to others the ruin it makes.'

'Well, then, power over ourselves, perhaps?' I spoke as mildly as I could, because I saw the black night of her severity descending again.

'Ha! You, too! You, too! You come to judge me like the rest!'

'I assure you, truly, I spoke with entire detachment, doña Teresa.'

'Then the words were put into your mouth. And that is worse – to me.'

She stood up, withdrawing herself from human touch, again.

'I assure you, I would never willingly pain or distress you, doña Teresa.'

'Ah! It is not what we do willingly, but what we do unwillingly, that does the real harm.'

'I don't think I understand you, doña Teresa. But I am sure that so far as it is in my power I would never return your kindness to me with anything but gratitude.'

It was the guitar that untuned the growing harmony between us. Its dusty, neglected condition roused my curiosity as I was examining the stock of instruments in an old shop in an alley-way behind the Cathedral. I thought it might be cheaper than the others I was shown, and was therefore surprised when the man asked a price considerably higher than I had expected, though I was bound to agree with him when he pointed out the evidence of its age and fine workmanship. However, he made no attempt to dust it up nor to let me sample its sonority; it almost seemed that he was reluctant to sell. This, naturally, made me more interested than ever. In the end, I bought it. and waited some time sitting by the counter while his boy restrung the guitar for me and found its heavy old wooden case on which had once been painted a name I could not decipher, it had been so thoroughly erased, probably with a knife.

But when I tried to discover the name of its former owner the shopman was quite uncommunicative, nor would he tell me whether it was of local make.

'The señorita is not superstitious, surely!' he said.

'Not particularly. But why do you ask that?'

'Because you seem to want to know about its past, and superstition is always a matter of past events or beliefs, is it not, señorita?'

'Well, yes!'

'But the English are too good at business to bother about such nonsense, unless they think it may take something off the price.'

'Oh, we are prepared to pay well for a touch of romance, all the same.'

'There is no romance about this instrument, señorita.'

'So you insist. Nevertheless, I suspect it of having had an odd past.'

'Only old women's tales, señorita.'

'Ah' I retorted, as he shrugged his shoulders, 'All the same, I don't see why I shouldn't have those tales, since I have paid a good price for the guitar itself. I would even pay something extra for its story.' This seemed to sting his pride a little. 'You have got a very fine piece of work there. It would fetch a great deal more without the story round its neck, if you would like to know.'

'You mean you bought it cheap yourself on account of its history?'

'I took a chance, señorita, that was all.'

'Well, I will take a chance, too, señor. Is it unlucky, do you mean?'

'Only to those who choose to think so. It came from the Duke of Coello's collection when all his stuff was dispersed. It has not been played on for half a century, we were told. The past is over and done with! There is not much more than that, except something unlikely about its previous owner having killed his wife in a fit of jealousy as she was playing it one evening.'

'Oh! I wonder what she was playing?'

'Who knows? Its too absurd, of course, but the legend is that it brings out the true nature of those that play it – the hidden fault, the human flaw, the ruling passion!'

'And nobody dares to buy it? I see!' I began to feel stirred with something like excitement as the boy carefully laid the guitar into its case. It was mine!

'Well, the señorita is too young to have developed a ruling passion, so all is well, I am sure,' said the shop owner, a little maliciously.

'Oh, I have a passion for beautiful sounds and rhythms. But we shall see,' I concluded, picking up the case.

As I left the dark little shop, I caught a corner of the case against the door. It was heavier than I had supposed and I carried it awkwardly. A muffled groan reverberated within. I stopped. But all was still. These silly, silly tales! A shivering sigh ran up and down the strings and I stopped again to listen and to let the vibrations of that knock subside. Did the guitar sense that it was coming to life again? If it is true that birth is often more painful than death, how much more painful must the experience of a rebirth in a conscious state! When I got back to the Villa there was nobody about. This was unusual. So I sat down in the sala instead of going straight to my room and carefully undid the heavy clasps of green-encrusted brass, then lifted out my treasure. I began experimentally tightening up the keys and began searching to run my fingers up and down the open strings, producing a shuddering glissando.

Suddenly I was aware of someone peering through the dim glass door of the little alcove where the canary hung in its cage above Tio Francisco's rush-seated low chair. The old man had been left on guard, I thought. I went on with my tuning, and slowly the door handle turned and Tio Francisco came out. At first I paid no attention to him and he stood stooping in the doorway, watching me. All at once I heard a rather horrible low gurgling. This made me look up sharply. But it was only the old man trying to express his pleasure in a chuckle which cost him exorbitant struggles. He came a step nearer, then another, and halted about two yards off; peering down on me. I went on stretching the strings, and he began to make uncouth gestures as if in mimicry, I thought, at first. But gradually I saw that he was try-ing to show me something, the way he would tune a guitar. And he began to mumble rapidly and to draw nearer with more insistent ges-tures. I felt inclined to borrow Teresa's manner with him, to tell him curtly to go away. But that was not my right to do. I looked up, how-ever, to show my wish to be left alone and I caught the full glance of his light blue eyes. The expression in them was compelling, the expression of one who has been wandering, lost over a vast tract of time and has suddenly seen a mirage across the desert. He held out his shaking arms.

'Ah no!' I cried, fearful for my prize. 'You would drop it!' I explained. But still he held out his hands and continued to stare with that dreadful, fixed longing. He was shaking slightly all over and I noticed how he sucked in the corners of the right side of his mouth to draw back the saliva as it oozed up under the stress of his excitement. I had never seen Tio Francisco like this before. His light blue eyes became more fixed, nearly ferocious with the determination to hold the guitar in his grasp. I grew uneasy. He was an old man. He might have a fit, I thought in alarm, what should I do then, alone with him in the house? Well, he could hold it for a moment, if he wished. I would keep close watch. It was hardly likely he would do it any injury. He saw me falter and gave me no time to hand it to him for-mally, but snatched it from my arms, with an exclamation almost of frenzy. At once he became alert and sure of his actions, not at all an impotent old wretch.

'Why you know how to play, I believe!' I cried, rather relieved at these signs of sanity. His fingers were flying from key to bridge and back to the keys again. And as if substantially restored to articulate life, he said with determined clarity, but slowly:

'There was no finer player in the army!' and resumed his tuning.

'Oh!' was all I could say.

'Yes!' No finer player in the whole army! My captain said I saved the campaign the night I kept the post awake, simply by – this!' and he chuckled with an eerie ghostly thread of a sound, then became intent on the guitar again. 'They never slept when I chose to play.' Speech left him helpless again here, but I watched him now without a word. He plucked a phrase, he throbbed a chord, then he hovered uncertainly, consciousness beginning to waver and recede to senile impotence once more. I leaned forward.

'Play me something, Tio Francisco. Play as you played for the army that night when you kept the sentry-post awake' I urged him. He stared up, vacant and wandering for the moment. Then the guitar seemed to stir the life up in his veins again and he whinneyed and neighed with delight. 'Ah-ha! Ah-ha! I will play! I will play! ' he promised. Then he drew a hand across his face as if to pull away a mist of cob-web tanglement and I realised that when he dozed as I had seen him doze so often, it was of a guitar he dreamed, a guitar that once he played, the finest player in the army. I wondered what he would play, whether it would be recognisable.

It was not what I expected. I had never heard anything like it. I never suspected a guitar could give forth such sounds. There was no formal melody or rhythm. Tio Francisco made of it a stage, on which his fingers produced shadow figures of human and animal characterisation, figures of sound, not of speech. It was not high drama. I began to understand, when once my mind and ears had grown accustomed to the novel use of the instrument – (though the tradition was old enough, I afterwards learned, one of the 'hidden' traditions of past times) – that it was very low theatre, indeed, burlesque is its politest title – and when Tio Francisco added the note of his own voice, howling like a dog, hiccoughing as a drunken man, imitating the enticing murmur of a woman, it plumbed depths I had only experienced once before at an Arab café chantant (so-called) where no Europeans cared to enter. It was obscene, I knew, and I should have stopped him, but it was inimitably done and not to be resisted. Tio Francisco had genius in his way. Perhaps it was a dying art and deserved to disappear. But it was an echo of something that had lived, lived in ribaldry and knavery, long, long ago. Here, was medieval burlesque entertainment started up to life again in a manner of performance that text-books and rare collected manuscripts are helpless to restore. I loved the echoes of that past most passionately, and lived in the imagination of what I could trace of it, in museums and libraries and in the tattered fragments of ballads sung by blind beggars and their gabbling boys.

I was so lost in this ancient world and in the picture added by Tio Francisco's figure of the Carlist bivouac, the soldiery through whose simple pastimes in the proximity of death the most vital streams of traditional entertainment are tenaciously kept alive, that I did not hear that step in the doorway.

Teresa swept in like a whirling avenger, black, harsh, and terrible as I had never known her. She took but one glance. The music stopped, and stopped, it seemed, to us, for ever. Menacing, with grim foreboding, look, she strode upon us. One instant she stood and the old man cowered. Then out swept her arm and crash! went the guitar, spinning, hurled to perdition, the look foretold. There was a ghostly cry and a wailing lament. Tio Francisco stumbled forward to save it in its fall. He might have saved himself but all his thought was for the guitar. He fell heavily, striking his thin skull against the iron base of the door. He lay where he fell and never moved. Teresa stood like stone, all the heat and rage gone out of her. I went to bend over Tio Francisco. I did not like what I saw. I turned to her, reading her thought immediately. 'He is breathing – I think,' I faltered. Then Felix hurried in.

'Ah! This has been due to happen for a long time,' he said swiftly, prompted by an angel. Teresa moved, then.

'Send Socorro for the doctor; I will hold him,' she said.

'No, no,' protested Felix. 'It is better to let me have him. It must have been a stroke. See the colour. Bring me water, señora!'

The doctor came. They carried the old man down to his room under the stairs. A little later the priest came. He stayed by the bedside and the doctor went away. There was nothing I could do. I went to my room and stayed there, listening, but the house continued very quiet. Later, Socorro brought me a tray of cold meat to my room. Even she wore a look of concentration to-night, and I knew by this that they were watching by the bed.

'Do not worry, sseññorita,' she said, almost softly for her. 'You can do nothing. He is very old, you know. Luis is there with Teresa.'

I knew I should have to leave. I sat up. But there was never a sound. I did not go to bed. But for hours there was no stirring anywhere in the house. Perhaps Teresa saw the light streaking out into the corridor from under my door. Perhaps she came on purpose. But I heard her stop outside my room at about three o'clock in the night. I got up quickly and opened the door, standing in silence before her. We looked at one another. But I could read nothing in her face and she said nothing in reply to the obvious question in mine. Then she came in.

'Why are you not in bed?' she said harshly. I shook my head and still looked at her.

'It was my fault!' I cried. 'It was all my fault.' And I burst out cry-
ing. She came over to the bed and sat besides me.

'No, no,' she said. 'No, no. You did not know. How should you?'

'It is my fault. I must go. I must leave you to-morrow. That is all I
can do, it seems. Forgive me, if you can. I shall never forgive myself.'

'What nonsense!' she said in a grating voice. 'It was inevitable. It
was bound to be. And I was bound to be the cause of it all.'

I looked up at her quickly. Her eyes were drawn and more staring
than usual and her lips flecked with white at the corners. I tried to put
my arms round her, but she put me by.

'No, no! You don't understand, Nana! How could you? You are
still a child, although you are the same age as I was when – when I
killed my father! '

'Teresa! '

'You need not look so horror-struck! It was not so bad as it sounds,
unless you choose to think so, of course! I tried to drown myself and
he tried to save me. In three days he was dead. From shock and chill,
that was all. But it is true what I said; I killed my father.'

'Why did you try to drown yourself?'

'Why do most people do away with themselves? Because they have
not the power to do what they wish, to have what they want more
than life itself.' The pressure of her emotion was rising steeply.

I took her hand and she let me hold it for a moment.

'Was your mother alive, then?' She withdrew her hand quickly.

'Yes. My mother was alive.'

Then her voice grew vibrant with a tenseness she could no longer
repress.

'I loved my father, but my mother hated me. Yet it was my father I
killed. He died in my arms. He said, as he was dying, he had said it
so often; 'She is so like my mother. She is so like my mother!' But his
mother gave him life while I brought about his death. Ah! That is
what it is to have the bad blood in one. But why in me? Why in

'There is no such thing, Teresa. Some have strong natures, some
weak, that is all. And circumstances decide whether the strength shall
be controlled or violent. Its the way experience makes character out
of nature, surely.'

'No, no. There is bad blood and it runs in families. It is true! It runs
in ours.' She stopped talking and drew herself up. 'What am I saying?
It ran in ours. It runs in our veins. And now at last it is nearly wiped

out. Only death and extinction does that! Well! It is nearly over. We die out and the blood dies in us. God Help us all! God Help us all! And I killed him, my father. That was the difference.'

'Dear Teresa! Your father loved you. How thankfully he must have died, knowing he had saved you.'

'Do you think so? I wish I did! But she hated me. And he knew it! My own mother hated me! Ah! You can't believe that! It is too unnatural! That was why I tried to do it.' There was a smouldering sense of injustice in her voice.

'But why, Teresa?

'Yes, why should that be? She was much younger than my father and he gave way to her in everything! But since I was a child, it was always the same. She grudged me that because –' Teresa was now dragging and twisting her thoughts to the surface of speech. 'I see it all now, of course. I have seen it all a long time, thinking and thinking. But I could see nothing then, only feel, feel, feel! I was a child, trying to grow in my own way of nature – trying this way and that – and there she was, watching me at every twist and turning. I could not grow straight. She would not let me do anything so simple and free. So I must twist here and turn there, put out a leaf here, a bud there, and at every point there she was waiting, to nip it off before it might flower. And it was so easy! Everything I liked she had only to say it was bad for me. That was all she had to do, just to declare that everything I wanted was bad for me. So simple, to think of that! And she was my own mother!'

'And what was it you wanted, Teresa?'

'I was never allowed to grow so straight as to know that simply. All I want was to be – to be myself. And I did not know how, because she would never let me be!'

'Wanting to be – what kind of self?'

'I shall never know. But it something that was – here!'

She re-folded her scarf over her breast and by that gesture I knew that 'something' was not extinguished yet. 'Then they began to say I was violent. Next, that I was uncontrollable. Then, finally, that I was dangerous. And it was becoming true! Yet all the time I meant harm to nobody. I would have kissed the feet of anyone who would have shown what I ought to do! She would lock me up because my father would not beat me, even then. After that, I tried to run away. Did you ever try to run away, Nanita?'

'Why, yes. Most children do at times if they are at all lively. But I always crept home again when I was tired and hungry.'

'I never crept home. They had to find me. They found me in the cemetery one night with my basket of clothes beside me and my father knelt down and took my hand and prayed to his mother in heaven to watch over me when he could not. And I cried and he wiped away my tears and there were tears that ran down his cheeks too as he took me home slowly. But I lagged along, and did not wish ever to return! And then she said he was not fit to have charge of me, because he had taken me the week before to his mother's grave on her birthday, and that was bad for me, like everything else. And then –' she stopped and looked at me for a moment. Then with an effort she went on. 'When I said you were everything I would like to have been, I meant it. I loved music, too. She said my passion for it was unnatural – and that must be stopped. I used to learn poetry and recite it in front of the gilt-carved mirror in our little sala. She took away my verse-book and forbade me to recite again. She ridiculed my voice and my attempts at gesture, saying a dwarf like me should run away and join a circus, and mouth and mimic with the monkeys, if that was how I felt, and then they would dress me in a red-spotted yellow gown, if that was what I wanted. Yet she would not send me away to a convent which was what my father kept saying, though he did not want to lose me; but he saw how it was, and how I could not go on. She said it was my duty to remain at home – so that she might torment me whenever she wished; that was what she wanted. Perhaps I could have been happy as a nun. I should have begun by appreciating the peace and calm, and the rest might have followed. Yes. I believe I could have made a vocation – then!'

Not now, evidently, I said to myself.

'Yet, do you know, Nanita, in spite of all, Nanita, a man fell in love with me! ' Somehow I had known this would come. The story was so simple and this turn of events so natural, I thought.

'Surely that was the most natural thing in the world!'

'You would think so? He did not think me a dwarf, evidently! He looked over the white wall one morning and saw me picking the cherries. In a month he came to see my father. But of course she would not let it be. He had returned to his people for a holiday and to find a wife if he could like one among the girls of our place. But she would not hear of it. She could not say he would have been bad for me, which was what she secretly longed to say, because everyone knew his family, but she said it would be bad for me in Tetuán, which was where his business was fixed. She said I already showed signs of feverishness and poor health. So he was obliged to go away. He did not choose another girl from our place. I was glad of that, you know. But then they began to whisper that I was possessed and I was put on a strict diet to reduce the blood and the priest came and tried to talk to me, but it was she who got him to come and made public knowledge of it, so I turned my face to the wall and would not speak, and would have none of it. None of it! After that I was left to lie in bed alone. It was very hot that summer. All I know each day was the sun crossed the white walls of my room towards the afternoon and that then my father would come a little later and sit beside me and groan under his breath and would have drawn me to his breast, but I would not. I would have none of it, now, not even from my own father! It eased after nightfall, but I'd wake in the early hours and shriek with the realisation of what I had grown into, the twists and thorns and the ache and the staring emptiness before me. And I would dash myself down on the ground and long to be broken. But the ground held me – and would not give way. Then I would cry for a knife to let the black blood run out of me – it was like a slow bitter poison clothing up my life – the thick black blood they had changed my young red health to. I would cry out and search for a knife, but everything was hidden away out of my reach. And I would feel that black, thick blood choking all that was left of the love and hope and goodness in life for me. It was then I would pray for madness. Yes, I prayed for madness, but even that I could not have! Why do you smile?'

'I wasn't smiling, Teresa. I was thinking that proved an acute form of sanity to pray for madness!'

'There is a knife's edge where both meet, Nanita.'

'I daresay. But you were spared that, thank God! '

'Do you think I was possessed, Nanita?'

'Of what?'

'Of what they said – the devil?'

'We have ceased to believe in that in my country.'

'They say here it can still happen.' We looked at one another, then I took Teresa's hand. It was a little hand, quite warm and firm, not hard as one would have expected, and only slightly tinged with brown. The nails were prettily shaped and smooth.

'I think' I said slowly, 'I think you were possessed by a sense of your right to grow into a fine, strong young woman and that when you fought as you did you were fighting a battle without knowing it, for yourself, it was true then, but for other young women, too. Many English girls before you fought the same sort of battle for the same thing and suffered for it, so that girls coming after, like me, could go easily about what they were by nature intended to do.'

'Yes, I daresay,' she answered, impatient of my generalising.

'All the same, they said afterwards I was possessed when I threw myself into the water and that my father saved me only by giving his own life.'

'But do you think so, too?' She scarcely heard my words, she was so intent upon the picture graved upon her mind.

'I know that those three days when he lay in a fever not recognising me, and I was cold as a stone as the truth lay bare before me, were the worst days of all. He turned towards me just at the last and smiled as he had always smiled when I could first remember and I took him in my arms and we kissed as we had not kissed one another since my childhood.' She took her hand away from me, and walked up and down looking out on the terrace in the gathering twilight. Then she came back. 'But I have not told you what it was that finally drove me to the water and what she did! Let me see if you believe that! Listen! After it was decided I was not well enough to marry, he went away. Then one day I received a message by the washerwoman. She was my old nurse – absolutely trustworthy to me. Then a note. It was to arrange to take me away, if I agreed. He was to come back quietly in a month and I was to be ready and we were to go away together and get married elsewhere. It was arranged. And I waited and kept my secret to myself. I told nobody. I was very careful and showed not a sign or gesture of what I felt, but somehow my mother read my mind. It was not mere suspicion. She knew. Yet I was so careful and hid my real feelings from everyone – from everyone, believe me! One afternoon, sometime after he had gone for good, as everyone thought – she came quietly into the room behind me. I did not turn round. I knew who it was but I was busy wondering how many clothes I could take with me. And she knew it!'

'How could she know if you told nobody?'

'One can learn to hide one's unhappiness, but never one's happiness, I think! It hangs about the air around us. That happiness! There is a whole lifetime in which to learn to hide one's misery. But happiness; that is too rare, too short, too strong, perhaps, because it is the life bigger than oneself that come then. Don't you think that is so?'

'I don't know, Teresa, except that I have read that happiness is the Universal Law and unhappiness the Great Schism of the Spirit. That we are unhappy because we know we are not happy and must be unhappy in order to know and recognise happiness!'

'What talk! What talk! I daresay it is easy to talk and easy to read everything and swallow it whole, at your age,' said Teresa impetuously, sounding not unlike a child herself. 'But do not try to tell me that it is easy to suffer; that it is good to suffer. It is not so. It will never be so!' she broke out passionately. I could not bear the sound of her voice.

'I would never dream of saying so, Teresa. You must not think that of me.'

'Well, do you wish you had never heard my simple story?'

'You have not told me the whole, yet.'

'Ah, yes!' She sat, gloomily contemplating the straight, iron gates below us, outside the window.

'What happened when your mother came into the room and stood behind you?'

'I always waited for her to speak. I had done so for a long time. So I waited again. She stood behind me and I waited; I waited a long time. Then, all at once, I felt a chill descend upon my back. A shadow passed over my head. I could feel it. I shut my eyes. I felt her hands laid tight upon my head. I was paralysed with the fear of her hands. She and I had not touched each other for many years. Tighter and tighter she gripped me round, pressing on my temples and my forehead. I could not move. Her hands were cold as ice. At first I almost fancied it was the touch of one who lays a blessing – but this was not a blessing; it tightened, it gripped my brain. It was a curse. I knew it! And all the spring in my thoughts congealed and withered – yes! at the touch of my mother's hands. I screamed out. I called on the saints and angels. But it was too late. They could not save me. Nothing could save me! My own mother had cursed my life!

'I rushed from the house, leaping and stumbling down the hill, crying out and wringing my hands. Then I saw the water and prayed it would accept me and take me to itself, not like the earth which only heaved one back to life. After that, it was the end; the end. It is still the end. What has come after is without sense or meaning. There was the funeral; then the friends departed and there was the emptiness of the house. I was alone with my mother. And still there was worse to come!

'On the day *he* should have come for me, word came to his family that he had been taken ill. I waited. Word came again. He had taken a cancer and I knew he was making arrangement to make another journey – alone – without me, and that was why he sent no word to me. He never wrote. There was no other message. Later, there was *his* funeral. I was early to meet him there in Church and I stood where he should have been standing to meet me. And they brought him in on their shoulders. Even that day came to an end. Then my mother took ill, in her time, not quickly, but slowly it came to her. Ten years slow shrivelling, and I nursed her. I was not permitted to nurse those I had loved and who had loved me, but I nursed the one I hated and who cursed me, and I was careful not to hasten her death, for in spite of the pain towards the end she did not want to die. I was out of the room at the moment she died, so I do not know what was in her mind at the last, or whether she saw my father or anyone else waiting for her, as they often do. And only then was I free, if you call that free-dom when you no longer care!'

'Well, he will live, the doctor says. At least, he will live a little longer.' she said with a sudden flatness of tone.

'Ah! Thank God!' I said. And again. 'Thank God! ' She did not join in with me. But after a moment she took my hand.

'So you are not to leave us yet, Nana, unless of course you wish.'

'I do not wish to go, if you would let me stay.'

For the first time, our cheeks touched, though we did not kiss. It was as if we together seeking human comfort from each other. And that was all. She went and I went to bed.

'Felix' I said suddenly after dinner the next evening. 'Will you see that the canary gets its flowering grasses sometimes? You know, the ones *he* always managed to find up in the hills?'

'Yes, yes, señorita. But don't worry about that. doña Teresa will see to it.'

'Oh', I said, a little doubtfully, for we all knew she would never go near the canary, nor take any notice of it except when it sang too well.

'Ah, you don't know! She will see to it.' he spoke with certainty.

He looked over his shoulder, then came nearer to me and bent down over the table. 'I saw her this afternoon. Do you know what I saw?'

'No, Felix. Tell me, do!'

'Why' – he paused and again looked over his shoulder then whispered carefully – 'She went into the canary – she didn't know I was watching or could see and put a lump of sugar between the wires of the cage ... And, you know, Tio Francisco has always to share his own piece of sugar with the canary, and there she was, giving it a whole lump to itself!'

'Ah! Did she? Thank you for telling me, Felix.'

'The canary will get its grasses as usual, you may be sure. Though I shall be ordered off to find them, of course.'

'Then – Tio Francisco will never recover sufficiently for that?' Felix shook his head sharply once or twice and drew his breath audibly between his teeth. 'Not for that, señorita. Why, he used to walk for hours and hours, searching for the special patches where those weeds grow! Well! He can sit in the sun for a while longer, the doctor said this afternoon. And who of us could be discontent with such a reprieve of nature? Socorro's aunt has already been ordered to kill a chicken for his soup tomorrow. A chicken for Tio Francisco's bowl of supper! Imagine it, señorita! Well, we shall get the bones, I daresay, and shall there be complaint? Not from me, señorita, not from me!'

'Doña Teresa has a strong sense of duty, I have begun to realise – with all the charitable things she does. She is never idle, is she?'

'Duty! Señorita, if you will permit me to say so, duty is a hard, meaningless word people use for something which is not hard at all.'

'Don't you find it so, Felix?'

'No, but then I don't make the mistake of calling it duty.'

'What do you call it, then?'

'What it is, señorita! The compulsion of our love of God drawing us all near together through the serving of others. And it is there working all the time, even through doña Teresa, though she refuses to admit it, like many others.'

Children on a Northern Shore

'THE CHILDREN ARE COMING,' CALLED Felix cheerfully, when I appeared for breakfast one morning.

'The children? What children?' I asked. I had been wakened earlier than usual by the sound of scrubbing of floors overhead and Socorro had been rushing in and out of the forecourt banging and beating rush mats and strips of carpeting for an hour at least.

'Oh, the *colonia* – the same that always comes – that is, different children, of course every year – but always the *colonia*.'

'A colony! To this house?'

'Yes. They fill all the attics and the lower courtyard room, also.'

'But – a colony you said! Are there so many of them, then?'

'Why, there are always more than enough! Not that I intend to criticise. After all, they are sick children, you know. Never less than twenty, though.'

'Indeed! We shall be lively! Or do we become a hospital?'

'No, no. It is not as bad as that! They are only weak, not really ill, though the doctor is always in charge. He comes for a free holiday, you see! And the three auxiliaries, they are always the same, more or less, that is, one professor and two assistants. They come for the sea air and to breathe a little, right the way from – from' he waved his hand vaguely towards the interior of Spain – 'where there is nothing but sky and bare rocks, and heat and thirst.' He put out his tongue to illustrate his words. 'Think of it, señorita! No water! We are lucky here. And because we have good water we also have good milk, and since we have milk we have butter, and then, since we have good cows we have good bulls also, according to nature, and fresh meat – and as for our fish – well, we have good deep salt water as well as the fresh. While there' – again he waved his hand in direction of inland Spain – 'there they have nothing but bad smells, so they say. Pssst! The ways of God are strange. To him that hath, shall be given, you recollect, señorita?'

'Yes, yes. So they come here to escape from all that. Does doña Teresa mind having them every year? Do they stay very long?' It is she who invites them before the season begins in mid-July. It airs the beds, as she says and the rooms and we all wake up after the winter and become busy again like the rest of the world.'

'When you say they are sickly children, do you mean anything serious?'

'No, no, señorita! Don't preoccupy yourself with ideas of contagion! There is nothing like that! Only perhaps a little cough, or a catch in the breath, or a faintness in the heart, or – or a softness in the bones – a twisted leg, watering of the eyes, and so on.' Felix exhausted his very inexact knowledge of anatomy before he stopped enumerating the various ailments we might expect to find in our coming guests; his gestures were somewhat misplaced, with the exception of the heart, which he pressed with great feeling.

'Ah! We shall be very lively to-morrow, señorita.'

'I see. Then the children are the swallows that foretell San Roque's summer season!'

'Exactly! Exactly!' Felix was pleased with my simile. 'Have you heard the explosions on the sands this morning?'

'I wondered what it was. I feared your revolution might be on the way.'

Felix did not like to hear that word spoken. He shook his head at me. He did not find this simile so apt.

'What are they blowing up on the sands, then?'

'The rocks. To make more room for people to sit on, I suppose. The numbers are greater every year. This summer they say the King will stay a whole month with the Royal Family, but I doubt if that is true. They usually stay six weeks before going on to Santander and San Sebastian.'

'Perhaps you will earn your bicycle in Spain, after all, Felix'

'Ah, señorita, you mock at me!' Felix said reproachfully.

I sauntered down to the beaches. Yes, they were blowing up the rocks, laying small charges, setting them off, then digging up splintered heaps of black rock and carting them away. Corporation officials, wrapped in ochre-coloured overalls were painting up the royal bathing saloon, shaped rather like an opulent bandstand; others were fixing locks on the doors of the rows of public bathing-huts and refreshment booths. Carpenters were singing and sawing away and banging and hammering everywhere.

There were strollers about, even though this was a weekday morning. There were children playing decorously on the sands, too, attended by Asturian *nanas,* all of whom wore the same costume, whatever their size – the larger the woman the more highly esteemed she seemed to be – with fluttering, pleated aprons and streamers flying in the sea-breeze, white stockings, white canvas shoes and round lace caps pinned down to the coils of hair on the back of the head. Their charges were the children of local well-to-do families who lived all the year round in the providence, official dignitaries of the town. I could not imagine that the boys and girls of the Madrid aristocracy could be more charmingly dressed than these little provincials, or more elaborately involved in social ritual. Provincial dignity is strong in Spain. However small it may be, every regional town is only a lesser capital than Madrid itself to its inhabitants; the ceremonial of public and social intercourse is nearly as rigid as at the Royal Court, and this punctilious adornment and dressing-up of children has a grave as well as a gay significance.

But the curtain on the royal season was not to rise yet. We were only gathered in the wings, poor relations come to see the scenes set for the gala performances to come. These children did not bathe nor even paddle. The beach guardians were not yet in attendance, and one bathed at one's own risk, as the warning notices said. Oceanic monsters that bit and drew blood, leaving poison behind them, were still being dashed into the shore-shallows by the strong late spring currents; red-eyed octopus of great size, and great squids that squirted blinding liquid at you, enormous, glistening black eels, like sea-snakes, reputed to strangle men in their coils and drag them down under the water, were no strangers to this coast, so though the weather was growing increasingly warm and the pleasures of bathing were proportionately inviting, the local children prudently played high up on the dry sands and only ventured to explore the wet, sea-weed-strewn margin when Papa was at home on Sunday and could take one reassuringly by the hand. Nana, of course, was far too timorous, and knew too many tales of evil, fearsome monsters, that haunted the bay with the sole ambition of carrying off some disobedient child.

The fruit-vendors began to sigh over the heat. The butter-and-egg woman from the hills perspired as she set down her double baskets and mopped herself frankly under the arm-pits before beginning her bi-weekly haggle. Even the contending fishwives, a vituperative class on the whole, abusive of each other's trickery, agreed on one thing, to pray that San Roque would be pleased to send a cooler summer than the last, when the best fish went bad before you could reach your good customers. That must, by the way, have been a very torrid time, for five times a week the race between these hordes of rival women was the liveliest spectacle of the town. Freckled and yellow-spotted like the flat fish they carried on their heads, coarse-grained of voice as their ballast cargo of cheaper fare were coarse of scale, they presented all the enlivening, and some of the grotesque, features of an obstacle race in their endeavours to be first sellers of the night's catch. When the boats had been delayed by the tides which not infrequently happened round such stormy coasts – the first women could always make a peseta or two more than the later ones.

It has always surprised me that in their search for what they call the soul of Spain men have studied every aspect of Spanish life except the most revealing and most natural of all. They have told us of its women, its painting, its history, its soil, architecture, the stage, its mystics, the men of action and the rest. Yet they have ignored the most natural, because it is the most unconscious manifestation of all – its children, those half-souls of the human race, its pure essential spirit, unadulterated yet by individual experience. But though the sight of them is to be had for nothing in the streets and by every open door their magpie chattering may be overheard by anyone who cares to stop and listen, children seldom appear in Spanish literature; the boy in Lazarillo de Tormes is, I suppose, the outstanding exception and he is a male rogue in miniature. There was no place for the child upon the old Spanish stage – there were no boy players – except as a singing angel in religious shows. Only the painters Velázquez and Murillo in particular have set them down before us, the buds of grace upon the tree of life, but mute and unexplained, and so they have remained to this day.

Chance, however, planted me in the way of children wherever I went in Spain and though, luckily, I was young enough to play with them, I was also old enough to mark the differences which set them apart from other European boys and girls and I awaited the colonia's arrival with more than casual interest. As the rattling *camionete* bumped up the stony track to the Villa Heliotrope, the sound of dark,

This family photograph shows Jack with his sisters. Ann is on the left, Dorothy on the right, and Margaret ('Mabbo') and Barbara between.

The family home in Hampstead no longer exists. The watercolour of Flask Walk, where Ann played as a child and bought her first books, is reproduced by kind permission of the artist, Gillian Lawson.

The scene on the north coast of Spain is of the Ensenada del Camello, and was kindly lent by Turespaña and the Spanish Tourist Office, with the help of Sr Gonzalo del Puerto. The San Roque Ann refers to may be that at Santander.

A la inglesa nuestra amiga
que alegró nuestra Colonia
con amor y simpatía,
con esplendides sin límites
con lecciones y armonías,
Deseamos los colonos
hoy que celebra sus días,
que Dios la colme de bienes,
de salud, paz y alegrías.
Que el cielo español, le diga
con su recuerdo, los días
en que los niños de Oro,
con amor, la entretenían

Angela Rodriguez Fe Laguna

Marcelina Gonzales Petra este
Amparo Estébanez Bernarda de
Presento Oncalaa la Torre
Adela Gallego Natividad
Felisa Sevillano

Made in France

The children's postcard records their
message and names. Ann evidently
treasured this.

Pau Casals at his house in San Salvador (El Vendrell) *c*. 1934.
Courtesy of Fundacio Pau Casals with the help of Sr F. Parcerises and Professor A. Terry.

Ann in her concert dress, Lisbon *c*. 1945.

Ann herself liked this passport photograph. Joaquín Rodrigo, who could hear but not see her, called her his 'maja inglesa'.

The drawing of J.M.W. Turner's house Sandycombe Lodge, Twickenham, was made in 1814 by William Havell. The original, which differs slightly from the engraved version, is in the possession of Harold Livermore.

The last photograph is at the gate of Sandycombe Lodge.

tense chanting rose to our ears. This was not the first, nor was it to be the last time my acquaintance with new young friends was heralded by singing. The colony had seen the sea for the first time in their lives – they might never see it again – this was their way of greeting it. No inducement was put upon them by their teachers to sing so publicly. Exhortations to display their scholastic community in song in the manner French and German teachers are wont to make would have been wholly unnecessary, since their outburst was an entirely spontaneous expression of feeling and quite unpremeditated. The pitch seemed very low for children's voices, but to them it was at the moment quite natural. That first sight of the sea roused in them a primitive, fierce exaltation deeper than the shrill surprise of children accustomed to annual outings. But the more normal shrill chatter as of starlings burst out when they jumped down from the camionete, swinging their travelling sacks drawn over their shoulders by cords, and clambering up the steps poured into the house and along the corridor where the savoury smell of soup promised an earthly benediction after the long journey of a day and a night.

I kept out of the way that evening. The children were put to bed immediately after supper and their teachers and supernumerary assistants seemed to follow soon after. Only the teacher in chief and the doctor sat up with Teresa detailing the circumstances of their journey and the more urgent problems which the visit inevitably suggested. I passed and re-passed the 'colonia' on the sands the next morning. On the following morning I went down with them to bathe. The boys glanced at me frequently with curious but friendly eyes; already there was competition among the girls as to who should carry my bag, my book, my bathing wrap. By the evening I was Nanita to children and teachers alike. By the third day they had evolved their own name for me 'Nanananita' with a cadential rise and fall of intonation I have never forgotten, and I had their names by heart. After a wet evening spent singing round my piano, we became inseparable companions. These were the names of the children:-

Angela; Fé; Marcelina; Petra; Amparo; Bernarda; Presenta; Adela; Natividad; Felisa; Julia; Agustina; Ángeles; Benita; Juana; Tránsito; then Manolito; Manolo; José; Manuel; Marcial; Bernardo; Lorenzo; Marcelo; Juanito; Joselito; Pedro; Jaime.

They were of pure Leonese stock, stirps – the word has not died out with them as it has with us – as Bacon would say, of that venerable kingdom from whose laws and high traditions the centralising force of Castile drew the strength which made it the standard bearer of Christian will through Europe and shaped a New World. They were wholly unspoiled, descendants of generations of artisan workers, carpenters, masons, millers, wheelwrights, smiths and so on. Quite a considerable number of them were fair-haired, though not very light of skin – about five in twelve – and these children had almost colourless eyes, like grey glass from which the sea has washed its original hue. I could not detect any superior characteristics in either fair or dark boys and girls as groups. Physically the fair ones seemed more vulnerable to nose and throat weakness; the darker-complexioned more liable to the tell-tale up-and-down susceptibility to feverishness. But in spite of a softer, slower mode of speech, the fair children permeated the whole with a solidity which responded amenably to kindness and reason; in the others there was a latent obstinacy which on sharp occasion would treat with nothing except total surrender to their point. This was a wild streak which no wisdom could direct and I did not envy those who had the controlling of them. Anarchy, I learned very quickly, was a vital instinct, not an intellectual principle, in the *colonia*. By our standards, the children were restless, quickly tiring of one game, particularly of organised sports In teams, and they were forever breaking up into groups of twos and threes in search of other pleasures and experiences. Their teachers were hard put to it then to get them together again; the girls would sit and sew for a while in company, because the material results were obvious enough, but the boys could not be held by that sort of ruse. There were not enough of them for 'futbol', the only modern solution ever found for this oldest of all Spanish problems of how to create and maintain unity without force. It was only on Sundays when Felix and other local lads kicked about with them on the sands that I ever saw one game continued to a genuine conclusion.

Their ages ranged from seven to eleven, except for the doctor's son, a hearty boy of thirteen, but they had no enthusiasm for make-believe. On the subject of fairies even the youngest were blank and uncomprehending, wrinkling up their noses at the thought of such absurdities. Not even Fé, who, true to her name, tried hard to believe everything her elders told her, nor even Felisa, who liked to please everybody, showed any desire to learn more of English fairy-land. Freaks and grotesques, monstrous distortions of the familiar human shape, in these they showed a morbid and quite unsympathetic curiosity. Mermaids, too, and ugly little men hob and goblin, witches, of course; they knew all about these, for they could still be seen. But fairies, winged flower spirits, oh no! But then they had never got up early on a fine June morning to clinch the argument by the sight and evidence of fairy rings upon the lawn of an English village green. In parched Leon and Zamora there were no green gardens where fancy's child could search out and imitate the humble bee, nor forest glades to stretch and deepen midsummer's imaginings. Stories to please these boys and girls must be of knights and giants, vorpal swords in hand, fighting for ladies in a perpetual distress but who nevertheless possessed the clue to some vast treasure-trove. Treasure and rewards these must be. They had not yet reached the class in school where it is made a point of orthodoxy to believe that Cervantes killed all that nonsense in the Spanish mind, once and once for all. Certainly the old chivalric tales were very much – alive to them, though they never attempted to enact these stories among themselves. When left alone they turned to practical things, to making things, if possible, little realists that they already were. Undoubtedly the happiest hours of the week were those spent clambering up and down the slippery wet rocks, peering into the salt sea pools for edible shell fish and vegetable samphire, and it was the consummation of joy and pride when any of these specimens were passed as eligible to go into the cooking-pot for the Thursday or Sunday *paella*. What a pity this natural desire of the Spanish child to make an individual contribution to the communal stock-pot is not zealously fostered and recognised for what it is – a potential force to make Spain a fruitful land again.

Those children on a Spanish shore gave more than one unconscious lesson to their elders. They had their own ways of settling quarrels, for quarrels of course there were, bitter and sudden. They were not concerned with making the punishment fit the crime, but intent on something far more difficult; a solution, in fact, of the temper of aggression in the spirit of forgiveness. The intervention of adult authority was seldom needed then and it always proved wiser in the long run to leave them to deal with their own delinquents on their own level. After all, they had to live and play together and that fact demanded more than a temporary expedient. Grown-ups can go home and shut the door upon neighbours with whom they had an argument. Not so the children, to whom play is the most serious necessity, after food and drink. The direct intervention of adult authority was seldom needed in these affairs, though in this particular colonia, a guiding hand was always ready.

Petra, the eldest girl, whose dark, stormy beauty seemed overlooked by her contemporaries and elders, – their preference, I noticed, was for the rarer types of pale, if not fair complexion, – had viciously whacked Tránsito across the knees with Tránsito's own spade and not only broken the skin but the spade, too. This was not only a crime against Tránsito, but against the colony; the skin would mend, but not the spade, and we could only muster seven spades between us. So while Tránsito wept for the blood which flowed, there was an angry clamour among the rest and Petra fled from the consequences of her wrongdoing and refused to come back when called but only wandered further and further away. It was at once and unanimously decided that she should be left outside the colony till she herself sued for re-admittance. The afternoon wore on; two hours went by; she was seen in the distance but tacitly ignored. Three hours passed. Socorro came down with the cloth-covered basket containing our merienda. Petra approached a little nearer, so that we could not mistake her presence. We sat in the usual circle and the ham rolls were doled out. She stood stock-still and watched our munching.

You get very hungry by 5.30 when the day has been spent in and out of the water in that strong sea air but we made no parade of our enjoyment. That was quite unnecessary. Petra's share lay in the basket. Only she could claim it. She made several dragging steps towards us, but we took no notice. Then someone – Felisa – suggested that Tránsito should be given the uneaten roll. 'I don't want it,' she said hastily, and could not help looking at Petra, now within earshot and whose defiance was melting fast into a crestfallen sullenness. 'Well,' said doña Isabel at length, 'You may as well take the basket and the bottles back, Socorro, thank you,' for we had all finished.

Tears were in Petra's eyes now, but still she could not speak. It was Tránsito, the wronged girl, who could no longer restrain her pity. She jumped up and made as if to draw Petra back into the circle before it was too late. 'No! No!' shouted the boys angrily. 'She has to ask pardon! She must ask pardon.' They were determined. Tránsito was obliged to withdraw. She had broken the tribal rule.

Petra gulped down her sobs. She was older than Tránsito, older than them all; indeed there was already signs of girlhood upon her, and these were still children. But still she was one of them and must conform. The final stage of the struggle was brief. She looked round the circle of hostile faces. There was no weakening there. Fortunately, Tránsito's head was downcast, hidden by her straight falling hair. That made the act of submission not quite so difficult. Petra muttered one last impatient exclamation, then took the last steps hurriedly. She turned towards Tránsito, and knelt on the sands before her. Then she put her hands about Tránsito's ankles and clasped them with a gesture of half-unwilling supplication. But for the final act of submission still they waited. She had to go on. They would not relent. With half a sob, she bent her face down again and while her dark hair swept the sands she kissed Tránsito's foot in total abnegation. The kiss unlocked her pride and she burst into tears. Tránsito took her in her arms, cried too, but only for a moment, and soon it was over and Petra was restored and Socorro went home with her basket, empty as usual.

This sort of incident was repeated several times, with minor variations, during the whole of their stay. In a simple way, these children showed that given absolute individual equality of right and a total absence of all privilege – doña Isabel's infallible impartiality as a Final Court of Appeal guaranteed that – the Spaniards could govern themselves wisely and well. The colonia reminded me without words that the Spanish people have the most acute instinct of justice, perhaps in the whole world, and it is the long violation of this primitive virtue which has reduced them to the miserable state in which they now exist.

When I was out of breath with running on the sands with the colonia there were always the teachers to converse with. There were three of them, between the ages of twenty and thirty-five, all unmarried. Two of them were certificated; the senior of these, doña Isabel, was a pale, handsome creature, with intelligent eyes, and the advantage, rare among Spanish women, of a softly modulated voice. Unfortunately, she was slightly lame. This was the only reason, so far as I could see, why such a superior woman should be found in such an insignificant situation. It was noticeable that on the rare occasions when she was absent, our conversation always sank to a level she would never have tolerated. But she was seldom away from her duties for long. Though such matters could well have been left to her auxiliaries, she was first up in the morning and never missed direction of the early plunge, as prescribed by the medical adviser. Each child had to be thoroughly ducked and submerged in the sea, so that the salt water should cleanse the eyes, the ears, the throat and nose. Isabel saw to it herself that no child ever escaped either then or in the evening ritual. She herself bathed in the middle of the day, alone, as well; I suspected that this was for her lameness. She had held several posts in more progressive parts of Spain, Barcelona, Valencia, Madrid. Why she had retired – for retirement it truly was – to such a remote province as outer Leon, I never ventured to ask, but guessed at some private disappointment which had altered, first, the inward course of their thoughts and then, inevitably, the outward range of her actions.

I was always sure of a welcome from Isabel whenever I appeared. She seized the opportunity of my knowledge of music and a world beyond Spanish limits brought for the instruction of her colony, though I was never pressed to talk in an informative way when once I made it clear that I was in a mood of supineness and wished for the time being only to lie motionless on the hot, bright sands and listen to the counterpoint of children's voices running in and out of the rhythm of the thundering waves beyond. She was absolutely impartial in distributing rewards or punishments and I never saw her fondle a child; yet she never checked their display of affection to the other teachers and she never discouraged the sudden, suffocating hugs of admiration with which they embraced me when she saw these were the only return I sought for the occasional pains I took to tell them stories or teach them songs.

When Isabel was not with us and the children were out of earshot, the conversation always turned upon men, and as invariably happens among Spanish women the talk was one long bitter complaint of the faults of the Spanish male. It always came down to one basic fault, the irremediably calculating, mercenary passion of his nature. A Spaniard would never marry a woman unless she had something, money, or its equivalent.

Saturnina, the auxiliary in chief, a not-unattractive tawny creature of thirty-nine – she looked fifteen years younger – usually took the lead in this sharp abuse, for though she had a short neck she possessed a very long tongue. She would dig her pointed teeth into her mouth with frustrated rage against the whole male sex. 'The world as it exists is solely for men, is enjoyment, but it was not made by man, in the first place', she frequently said. 'Women never find out till too late what it is all about. The young girls don't want to learn, I didn't myself, we are all sure of our power over men and advantage over the other women till we approach thirty, and then it is too late. They talk of conspiracies and revolutions in the papers and at meetings, but there is only one conspiracy in the world and that has existed since the beginning of time, the plot of men to make society a system in which women are exploited entirely for man's advantage. One day there will be one more revolution and it will be a real one, because it will be the last – the revolt of women against men! Would to God I could live to be in it!'

'But how will you bring that about, please?'

'If you want to get the money you will have to do the work,' said the youngest teacher, not unwisely, I thought.

Saturnina turned on her. 'We do all the drudgery now!' she burst out, 'and still they keep the money. You know that.' Money did seem to be important to these people – it had a scarcity value, of course. Here Isabel's shadow, limping ever so slightly, glided over the sands and stood over us.

'Do you agree with every other Spanish woman, doña Isabel, that the men are the egoists of your race and the women the slaves?'

Isabel considered for a few moments. 'I can't speak for other races, of course, but I certainly agree that Spanish men are ruthless egoists and their relations with women.' She stopped talking while she shut down her parasol and I saw she did not care for the course the discussion had taken. Probably she was aware how monotonously constant it was as the main theme of women's talk, but adeptly she found her own way of lifting the topic to a more original level. 'I think, too, that it explains why great art is so rare in Spain.' She looked round in amusement at our surprise, as she sat down beside me. 'Oh yes, it is rare, you know; that is, when you think what we *might* produce, what we are capable of producing. Yes, I think one could make out a strong case against the extreme egotism of the Spanish male on those grounds.'

'That sounds interesting, but I can't see how it goes on. And then so far I have met comparatively few Spanish men,' I explained.

'No? Well, take your own country for instance, shall we?'

'By all means.'

'Well, "to make a fool of oneself" is a characteristic English phrase with which we foreigners are familiar, you know. It is very revealing, though you don't seem to realise that! It gives us a clue to your rather curious nature, for whatever his limitations, and we know more about them than you may think we do, it is well known that the Englishman is never afraid of making a fool of himself if he finds cause – I daresay he often makes a fool of himself for nothing at all, but I am no judge of that! But there it is. He will make a fool of himself quite willingly for something outside himself. Now that is something no Spaniard will ever do; it spite of don Quixote, who is, after all, our exception, our great freak, though the text books never dare to say so! It is true, isn't it, for instance that the Englishman will marry for love more often than not?'

'Oh yes, the average man would be ashamed to appear to do anything else. Indeed, I doubt if he would attempt to marry for advantage without some form of self-deception, persuading himself that he is half in love, at least, and that the rest will come – in its proper time!'

'Well, you have put it at its most cynical, but there it is, you agree! The Englishman will lose himself in something beyond himself, will try to lose himself and find himself in something bigger, and that is why, in my opinion, you have more original genius in England than we have in Spain, in spite of the fact that your climate deprives you of the natural conditions most conducive to the creating of great painting and music.'

'But surely you have produced dazzling quantities of great art in Spain?'

'Not what we might have, considering our natural advantages,' she returned with unexpected vigour. 'Oh we make a great noise in the world when we produce anything out of the ordinary, I know, but take away the attraction of our native way, which is so exotic to you that it diverts your critical faculty, and there is not so much, after all. In my own life-time I have seen genius dwindle into talent, not once but several times and always it was the same cause; the not-counting-the-cost, which is genius, dwindling and drying up into the calculating-of-the-expense, which is talent, and nothing more.'

Don Luis and two priests from the town were pacing along the sands beyond us at this point and Isabel took them into prompt consideration as she was looking out to see that all was in order within her colony. 'And when our men are not egotists they tend to become priests, and whether there is not a trace of a supernatural form of egotism in that, how should a woman know?' She dug the tip of her parasol into the sands, and traced a geometrical figure – a bisected circle – before our eyes. 'No!' she went on, 'in spite of all our fame and, I repeat, our natural advantages, we have no Shakespeare, no Angelo, no Mozart; they were not egotists, but we are!'

'You call Quixote a freak, well what of Lope and Calderón?' I said, determined to keep the discussion alive, at least.

At this Isabel threw down her parasol and wiped out the geometrical problem she had projected. She lifted up a handful of fine spun sand crystals, and let them fall very slowly through her fingers, intently watching their microscopic differences. Then she brushed the traces of them from her long, pale fingers.

'Nanita!' she said, and for the first time she spoke as though I were a tiresome child, asking a very silly question. 'I have read Lope and Calderón and all the rest of the great masters as prescribed by all our authorities without exception – one has to, you know, to become a teacher – and I have marked and digested, I hope, all the beauties they contain, but do I truly care if I never read them again? Nanita, I do not! And why? Well, I can only suppose they have made no lasting impression on my heart, though that, you must remember, is a woman's heart, and strutting and *prosing* however grand the torrent of words, make no effect there! They are only parts of a whole and therefore they are not part of me. There are things in English, many things in French — ah! without them, life to me would be infinitely the poorer, infinitely the more wretched, even by the loss of recollection alone — but, frankly, if someone made a bonfire to-day of the books which have appeared in Spain since Quixote's curate and the barber burned his old library – I might except one or two rare spirits, perhaps – really, I should be too indifferent to make any comment upon it!'

The youngest teacher looked frightened and horrified, but dared not speak. Isabel was so much our superior in intellect and experience. A slight chill of depression settled on us.

'NO! They are not part of me; they never were. They have not grown in me, or with me. Is that my fault? Well, then, so be it! Even our painters, and there, it seems, is where our best talent lies, – Greco? Yes, of course! But he was not a Spaniard, and his style was formed before he came to us. Neither was Velázquez, you know. His warmth of humanity and his love of human character undoubtedly came from his Portuguese mother's side. His technique may have been Spanish, I allow. But those Portuguese! Lope was right! You remember what he said about their vehemence? Yes, they have kept the *folie du coeur,* and its receptivity, for which we ridicule them, idiots and egoists that we are, because we have cast it out of our souls. Have I said enough? There is another thing; not the production of abstract works of art, but the practical art of making noble lives of ordinary men and women, the real art of living creation. What would you say was the supreme test of that in a people, Nanita?'

I looked round at the lively, glittering scene about us; at the early visitors bobbing up and down in the waves; at the yellow-clad shore-guards striding on the margin of the beach, or pulling on their oars a little out to sea beyond the breakers; at the soldiers and the Civil Guards; at the little knot of priests, now sitting on the rocks, at the nannies and then at the children.

'The children?' I suggested.

'Of course Nanita would say that! ' said Saturnina. They all laughed.

'They are the most beautiful children in the world to look at,' I said stoutly, 'always loving and always loveable by nature. They are your finest product.'

'Good! ' replied Isabel. 'That brings me to what I was going to say. Yes, our children are our most wonderful product, and see what a miserable misuse we make of the material when we have it in our hands! Look at our old people and compare them with the little ones. Our beginning and our end! Do you have such dreadful sights of misery and bitterness to turn aside from in England, Nanita? No! Everyone knows your old folk are sound and wholesome, like your native apple! There is the test of a race and its way of living! And there, I think, I have answered your question. Egotism is our curse. It blights our children's lives as surely as it blights our other gifts of nature. There is drought in our souls and we cry to quench it with hyssop and vinegar.'

Again she caught up a handful of fine sand and let the grains fall slowly through her fingers. We sat rapt and attentive about her, not wishing to interrupt her thought. But she remained silent. So at length I venture to rouse her again.

'I have no reason yet so say so, but, somehow, I believe there must be many women like you in Spain, Isabel; Not so brilliant, of course, but with the same character, the same will. Perhaps the change is to come through you.'

'It must! It is the only way! Manolo! MANOLO!! Give that ball back to Juanita immediately! And come here! I have something to say to you.' All this time she had never forgotten where her charge lay. Manolo, the swarthy, squat, squinting boy came up from the water's edge as slowly as he dared, and almost at once we became a little court of complaint again in which Isabel was eternally admonishing, exhorting and generally administering justice and equity.

I did not willingly pry into people's minds or follow up clues they had carelessly exposed in the course of conversation, but never the less, it stayed in my mind that Isabel had seen a particular case of genius dwindle down to talent and had not liked it. I permitted myself to guess the rest.

'Yes,' said Teresa to me that evening when I introduced the subject of Isabel's superiority and expressed my surprise that she should have so modest and employment. 'Doña Isabel is an exceptional woman, we all know and the Princess was very disappointed when she refused her nomination to the royal girls' academy in Madrid last year. I don't suppose she will get another opportunity like that for a long time, perhaps never. Her Highness is growing very old. Patrons don't grow on every tree,' she added.

'Isabel prefers Z ...?'

'Of course not. Who would prefer that place to Madrid?'

Yes, I thought, I suppose it is in Madrid that one particular genius is dwindling down to talent, and Isabel prefers exile in Z ... rather than witness the sight of someone going the way of the others. Perhaps she thought the genius was very rare, probably she loved him. In the case of a more ordinary woman I would have ended such thoughts with the pitying sigh 'Poor Isabel!'. Isabel was no object of pity, though. She did not try to repress her emotional nature, like Teresa, but used it continually. She filled each day with action, so that she went quietly to bed at night. She never cared to stay outside and rhapsodize on the warm bright beauty of these early summer evenings. She found the scent of the heliotrope 'sofocante', 'too, too sweet' she told me once when she found me with my head drowsily buried in its twining blossoms under the climbing moon, and I had invited her to share my pleasure.

When St John's Eve came Teresa was very lenient with the children, allowing them to build a bonfire immediately behind the house in the clearing. This had never been permitted in other years, I was told. We spent happy hours gathering twigs and branches for our celebration of this old midsummer rite. Especially did we take joy in bringing home the laurel for the coming year, singing till the forests rang;

'A coger el trébole, el trébole, el trébole†,
A coger el trébole la noche de San Juan!
Ay! Ay! la noche de San Juan!'

Ay! Ay! la noche de San Juan, when we leaped over the rising flames as they crackled and roared, with mingled glee and alarm as some of the more daring boys endangered their flesh and singed their clothing by taking too close a jump; our dances round and round with hands linked, our songs and happy abandonment. This was the last relic of the tree –

'A coger el trébole, el trébole, el trébole,
A coger el trébole la noche de San Juan!

worshipping times of their ancestors in a land that had despoiled itself of the source of its primitive strength, material as well as spiritual, in the felling of its once great forests. Only the pine is left; the tree of solitude, as some of these northern songs call it; 'a pine tree to weep under in loneliness,' so they lament. Well, it is not such a sheltering friend, perhaps, as our own poet averred a tree should be, but still, to our little colonia the pine-woods brought fresh health and invigorating air and there were days now of such intense glare upon the sands that we were glad to retreat within their hushed, high eminence.

It was in their groves that we built our grottoes to Saint James, with the frames of cockle-shells to guard and sanctify our votive treasures, our beaded mirrors and tinselled ribbon gew-gaws, the coloured picture cards of the Sacred Heart and the Infant Jesus; a photo of the King on a polo pony, a 'silver' pencil and other hoarded offerings. And though no pilgrims to Compostella now passed along this ancient way, we knelt and sang our chants to Heaven in duty bound, primitive, strong little halfscale tunes, firm and tried and true enough to hold and contain the vague mysterious passions which shook our blameless hearts we knew not why, as they had shaken the

---

† Trébole is trefoil or clover, and the children are going to look for it on St John's eve.

spirits of generations long gone by and, please God! would stir and echo on through generations long to come.

St Peter, too, had his tributary songs. He seemed, by the awe and gravity of the tunes dedicated to his Day, to have given a special sense of protection to these little ones' forefathers and the shadow of that long belief still hung over the melodies as we in our turn sang with simple faith.

But the joys of these midsummer celebrations were saddened by the thought of leave-taking and a return once more to the pinched life of those sun-baked provinces.

Then, unwittingly, Anibal the parrot became the means by which that health-restoring holiday was prolonged as if by a miracle. For Anibal died, and his death was not in vain, since by that sacrifice the children's paradise was extended.

It was my fault, and it happened in this way. Once every other month or so the kitchen was thoroughly washed and scrubbed, the walls and ceilings scraped and whitened, the fire put out and the household reduced to cold fare for a space of twenty-four hours. It took a long time to dry out, for the kitchen was an inner room with no window opening on the outside world. At these times, Anibal had always sojourned in the dining-room until the damp air was sufficiently dried to allow of his safe return. But alas! on the day of June when this monthly scouring was begun, I had cause to put in some intensive work at my piano, for doña Clara was getting up a charity concert for the sanatorium above the hill and I had been asked to sing. There was a good pianist down in the town, one of your pounding sort, but with a buoyant, unshaken rhythm. He deserved a better lot than that of cinema pianist, and he knew it. He was therefore anxious to give a good account of himself as accompanist on this opportunity and though I was appearing only to give some sort of foreign interest to the programme, he was none the less anxious to prove ability as early as possible in rehearsing, possibly because it was rumoured that there was some hope that Conchita P might come on from Bilbao where she was delighting everybody with her natural presentation of regional songs in costume that eschewed the pedantic 'folclórico' but escaped the music-hall's glittering banality. I was sympathetically disposed towards his not very obscure aim, so doña Clara brought him up in a car to run through some possible items with me.

Poor Anibal was wantonly neglected. It was a wet day; he could not be put out to sun on the terrace and therefore he was left in the kitchen to moulder and shiver. I knew nothing about Anibal's plight. But it was unintentional carelessness; everyone in the house was excited, and the colonia, of course, hung round stairways, door and corners, trying to get glimpses of what was in progress in the dining-room. Anibal remained forgotten; all night he was left in the dank air, his discomfort aggravated by a draught from the open door. Next morning, while we were all at breakfast he gave a curious screech. It was obvious that something was peculiarly wrong. Felix ran immediately and found him lying on one side with one paralysed claw stuck grotesquely out. Nothing could mend its condition. No consolation was possible. He refused food and drink; he would not let even Teresa touch him, but opened and half closed his beak with a gasping flutter that was all awry. He grew worse and worse. His little heart scarcely moved except with intermittent jerking convulsion. The carbuncle on his forehead glistened as if with sweat. Only the eyes glared, immovably fixed. Then the sun came out and the canary burst forth with glorious song. Teresa turned on Tio Francisco as if she would rend him to pieces for this lack of sympathy with the agony of poor, pitiful Anibal. Tio Francisco cowered back and made off quickly. In a moment the canary was silent and we heard him no more that day, though the sun shone on and on and mounted hot in the heavens. But alas! it was too late to save Anibal. Why could the sun not have shone the day before? All day the parrot's agony went on. Teresa never left him. I sat in the sala by the door and waited. The rest of the household seemed surprised by my agitated suspense. At dinner that evening, as we were finishing, it was about nine o'clock, poor Anibal screeched again, again in terror. Everyone stopped eating. One or two children crossed themselves quickly. 'He is on his feet!' cried out Socorro. Felix ran out. Teresa was already there. Anibal was dead.

It was my fault, it was my fault entirely. I had known from the first that he was Teresa's nearest, indeed her only true companion. She had shown me great kindness, with a delicacy of feeling and understanding rare among Spanish women. And in return I had caused the death of Anibal. I fasted on the morrow, as I had fasted on the previous day. Felix threatened to tell her why I refused to eat but I forbade him with such stricken looks that he desisted.

But that night she must have guessed at my distress, for at some late hour she came into my room and found me sitting up in bed, staring out at the moon which was full again. She felt my forehead and went out again, returning with a linen compress soaked in vinegar which she bound tightly round my head. The vinegar trickled down my cheeks in drops but less pungently, less bitter than the tears I could not keep back now, though in my mouth the vinegar had a taste of aloes and myrrh.

'It was not your fault,' she said, taking my hand.

'It was,' I whispered back. 'If only I had known ...!'

'No, no. Love brings loss. Love is loss,' she tried to say. I did not ask her what she meant but laid my head on her shoulder and cried, till I grew more feverish still and my temples ached and throbbed. As I recalled every incident of Anibal's life and what he meant to her, my remorse became unbearable and I tossed and groaned to think of what I had caused.

Teresa brought the colonia's doctor, but I scarcely noticed him. We saw very little of him in the Villa, as he took the chance of visiting old acquaintance down in the Cafés of the town and seldom came to the beach. But he was amiable and easygoing, and came readily enough to see what could be done to quieten me. He made one or two ineffectual attempts to puncture my arm with his hypodermic needle, but it was blunt, and rusty too, I could have guessed by the roughness of its surface. It was my first experience of provincial medical practice in the Peninsula; however, he managed to give me some sort of relief. I lay back on my pillow and Teresa stayed beside me till I believe I fell asleep.

Anibal was not stuffed and set up as a household deity, but Teresa never spoke of him if she could help it. The perch was never seen again, and I noticed she never used the watering-can. But I observed a contraction of her brows when the innocent canary poured out a particularly joyous curve of melody, and she spoke to Tio Francisco on such days with an irritation she could not conceal. So he shrank back and seemed to adopt an apologetic air for what his pet and darling sang. And every time it sang, my thoughts, too, went back to Anibal and I was continually suffering from the misery of remorse and brooded on my guilty selfishness. The piano was shut and there were no more merry evenings with the entire colony crowded round it. The children felt the chill of my withdrawal, though I did not heed, the effect this had on them. They were leaving in less than a week but, as it happened their hurt and puzzlement did not go unnoticed else-where, fortunately?

One morning I went late in to breakfast, listless sand heavy-eyed. It was some minutes before I became aware of a stir of excitement and of smiles, nods and whispers. Then it came out. Teresa had invit-ed the colonia to stay till St Anne's Day! St Anne's Day. When was that? Oh, St Anne's Day!

I saw the meaning of this offer at once. And if I had not, the chil-dren's shining eyes would have made it clear. When Teresa came to the door, there was a murmur, then a shout of approbation.

'One more week!' they chanted. 'One more week!' They broke from their long trestle tables. They advanced upon me. There was an avalanche of hugs and kisses as though it was me they had to thank and not Teresa. 'St Anne's Day! St Anne's Day! Doña Isabel says we will hire a donkey and take you and our dinner with us right up to the light-house on your Saint's Day. The light-house! The light-house! On your day, Nanita! On your day!'

And I, who had never celebrated my Saint's Day in all my twenty-one years, had yet to learn its date. The colony was in a delirium of delight. I saw Teresa in the distance. I could not bring myself to go to her, to speak to her. But I looked at her with new eyes and a sensa-tion I could not define, and she saw the look and there was answer-ing affection in her eyes as she turned to leave the room.

'But how will you manage, with all your visitors arriving so soon?' cried Saturnina. 'It will never do. And the expense! You will never manage!'

But Teresa went away without a word. So Anibal's flight to the Paradise of Brazilian birds – was he hovering in spirit above the Amazonian tangle of forest and steamy swamp? – was uplifted on the happiness of little children, and on a benediction of love that flow-ered through the sorrow of his death.

That week passed swiftly as pleasant times do. The blue of the sky deepened day by day; the sunsets lingered and seemed to settle in the west. Even the weaker children lost that wan, pink-lidded look about their eyes, and the tight-drawn look of the skin that gave too sharp a definition of the skull to some of those childish heads was gradually effaced. We played in what seemed an eternity of ease within the shal-lows of the tides and the pools between the rocks.

St Anne's Day came. A birthday in the height of summer was a new luxury to me. When I got up that morning Felix ushered me out on to the balcony where a table had been set for one. I should have known it was laid for me in any case because of the sugared sponge-fingers and the tiny gilt casket heaped with wild raspberries and cherries. No one else in the Villa broke fast on such dainty fare. I was bending down over a bowl of low-cut roses, knowing well enough whose hand had placed them there on that particular day, when idly I sensed a flithering, whispering sound behind me. Before I could turn round two cold little hands were pressed over my eyes and I could see nothing.

'Guess! Guess!' went up a chorus of shrill, eager voices.

I went through each name of every girl and boy in the colonia, receiving an excited 'Si!'Si!' to each call, adding, after I had completed the recital. 'And it is Fé who is blinding me!' Suddenly I felt a trickle of some cold liquid pouring slowly over my head. There was a sweet smell and a merry outburst at my bewilderment. I looked up. Amparo held out a flask of perfumed oil. I had been anointed for the festival. The girls kissed me in turn; the boys shook me by both hands, bent before me with half-bowed courtesy.

Then Petra presented me with an envelope, followed by Joselito, who presented me with another. Inside each was an illuminated address in more or less identical words. They were:

> 'To our English friend who filled our colony with love and sympathy with her lessons and songs. On this her birthday, we pray that God may bestow on her wealth, health, peace and joy.

> 'May the Spanish sky (Spanish does not distinguish between sky and heaven) recall the days when the children of T ...received her with love.'

Now on St Anne's Day twenty years after, I return your greetings. I see you now as I saw you then, wearing your best overalls for the holiday, those blue-striped white linen uniforms, belted and bloused, and your canvas alpargatas newly whitened and threaded. What has become of those 'illimitable splendours' of which we were exultantly conscious? And has God showered on you, or on me, or on any of us those benefits, health, peace and joys of which you wrote in that message? Looking back on those intervening years, the wars, the suffering, the inhumanity of race and family to family, I do not wonder that silence alone answers my question. But Amor y Simpatia – love and sympathy – I feel those still, and so I trust do you in spite of the

malice and envy of a world which seems intent to strangle what nat-
ural kindness and hope of future goodness is yet left on earth. Amor
y simpatia! Those were our childhood's endowments. Let us keep
them still. Above all, I pray, that under the 'cielo español' by a mira-
cle of grace you have not lost that trust which shone in your eyes; that
trust in others which is the mark of childhood and alone made possi-
ble our contemplation and the sense of 'illimitable splendours'.

The donkey arrived. I clambered up. The boy cracked his whip –
someone had tied a blue riband on it – my colour, they said and the
creature strained his buttocks, and pulled with the cooking pots and
pannikins creaking and swaying round and about but always
upwards till we got as near to the summit as our lumbering pace
could stand. The lighthouse was our first thrill. Even on that hot
morning a cold wind tore and raged round the tower and snatched
away the exclamations out of our mouths as if to show what a puny
thing it was after all that we so much admired! From those dizzy
heights we gazed fearfully down upon the green enticing sea shad-
owed by the cavernous jaws of purple rocks, flecked with spume and
always hungry for the storm.

The mid-day meal was our next enjoyment. We had brought a
paella up in two enormous pannikins and quickly made our own
camp fire to heat the water for the steamers. The rice was formidably
rich; tomatoes, pimento, sausage black and white, mussels, bits of
crab and lobster, even, for the quick-discerning fork, and though the
pine cones hissed and spluttered and we never succeeded in getting a
clear red fire, our plates were tolerably free of smut and ash. There
followed melones, melocotones, albericoques, plátanos. Skins, peel,
pips and stones were burned in the embers and there we lay spread
all about upon a carpet of pine-needles while the next item was pre-
pared. This was a tribute to me; a concert of songs. 'Songs even you
have never heard,' said Isabel, with a smile. This concert lasted a
long, long while, for I wanted to hear each song twice – and two of
them three times over.

Then there were races for which I in turn had prepared a surprise
in the shape of prizes. At this announcement several children turned
quite pale with terrible determination. To win became a matter of life
or death. They did not race for racing's sake, or sport, as we vaguely
call it. They ran for death or glory; something of the spirit that
burned in Nelson when he cried to his seamen before going to battle

'Glory or Westminster Abbey!' was in the air. On the other hand, it was not for the prize's sake they raced, for they were all satisfied to find in the end that there were rewards for everybody and that every child had some keep-sake to cherish.

The sun was slanting ruddily through the pine-groves before we shook the pine-needles out of our clothes and began to load the donkey and gather our party together again for the return journey. The resin in the bark everywhere was welling up responsively to the long-drawn heat of a cloudless evening and tinkling into the resin-cans, nailed half-way up those tree-trunks which had been marked and gashed by man for sacrifice.

We sang all the way home while the evening dusk seemed to quieten all things else into a listening pause and the stars were out over our heads before we reached the Villa.

When I went down to the railway-station in the town with the *colonia* that next day, Fé held me tightly by one hand and Felisa on the other hand pulled at my arm. Ángeles squeezed in behind me in the *camioneta* and pressed her elbows round my neck so tightly that at sudden turns in the road I was nearly strangled in her clasp. Natividad had managed to grab my handbag in a little scuffle that had risen among the others, in which Petra had slapped Presenta with a hard vicious blow that had drawn tears and subdued threats of reprisals later.

Later! How our counting of time had hurriedly changed its numbers before the coming separation! Weeks had turned into days; days, too soon, into hours, and now those dread and faithless hours into treacherous, quick-sand minutes.

It seemed only a moment now before they were mounted high into the truck-like carriage of the cross-country tranvia. Already that puffing billy's high chimney was belching out lugubrious wreaths of black smoke and precipitating its rain of soot upon us. The steam was shrieking at terrific pressure. We could not hear each other speak. Perhaps it was better so. Our farewells could not be expressed in phrases. I was dragged up into the corridor and caught up into wild, long, last embraces. Scratched, torn, dishevelled, I was pressed close again thumping, thudding hearts. There was no weakness about these pulsations, thank Heaven!

'Venga con nosotros! Venga con nosotros!' cried the boys.

'Si! Si! Venga! Venga! Venga' implored the girls.

'Later! Later! I will come as soon as I can', I promised.

'I wonder if we shall meet again,' Isabel found a moment to say.

'Perhaps we may. I hope so.'

'And I, too,' she said. 'And I too.' Then she added: 'You will write?'

'Yes, and I will come when I can,' I promised again. We kissed each other on both cheeks and I descended. I could hardly bear to lift my head, but they were crowded round the windows now, waiting to catch a last farewell. Yes, they were all there. Well! It was a pleasure to see how different they looked now, tanned, invigorated, no longer weak and ailing.

The train lurched. Instantly, there was a boding silence. Slowly the train began to move, slowly, slowly, I was obliged to step along beside them. They looked down at me and now there was a look of surprise, almost of apprehension, on their faces. For them it was the first experience of the reality of parting, between those who, in spite of promises, may never meet again. This look almost of fear made me check instantly the tears that were threatening to roll down my cheeks.

Then – all at once, like soft evening shower, a consoling sound stole on my ears; softly, very softly, without any premeditation, they began to sing. It was the song I loved best of all, the song they had been chanting when they had arrived and we had first met, the reapers' song of harvest. I had to walk faster now, faster, faster. And now we were apart, asunder; the distance between us grew longer and longer. Then it was no longer a distance; it was a gulf. I could not see the expression on their faces, nor could they see mine. They sang more loudly now, as the rising chant possessed them. Then even the sound of that grew fainter and they were gone.

Twenty years ago, that was. Where are you now and what songs do you sing after all these years? What sort of harvest have you reaped from these intervening seasons? Some of you, perhaps, all of you, I hope, have children of your own, born in bitter times, rocked by the thunder of guns, wakened to the light of burning villages. Do you sing those songs to them? And do you sometimes recall the peaceful summer you spent at San Roque and tell them of the English girl who loved you then, and loves you still? And who would love them, too, for your sakes?

I turned aside out the station. The square was dusty, bare, deserted. But I could not face the Villa Heliotrope, empty now of eager faces, so I took my merienda at a dingy pastelaria on the corner. The sun went in. Torn sheets of a discarded newspaper blew disconsolately round about the pavement. Yesterday, men had walked five miles and more to read its news. Now, only a few hours later, and although the Madrid daily press had not yet arrived to oust it from its place in life, it was already staled, soiled and trampled underfoot into the gutter.

Dispossessed

ON THE FEW OCCASIONS THAT Don Luis left his seminary to visit Teresa, – and then, it seemed, only to tax the catechistical memories of the *colonia*, – he avoided me with some care. So I was somewhat surprised to hear that I was included in the invitation for Teresa to visit Comillas on his last day as a fledgling priest.

There was a rarefied atmosphere about everything at Comillas. Before going to the seminary, Teresa and I climbed up to the 'venta' high over the sea, and there I drank half a bottle of the finest white wine I ever tasted; she would not drink, so I had it all. It was so rare, it did me no harm. We lunched in the open, to the left of that wide sweep of the Asturian mountains; the peaks were still covered with ice and snow, and before we descended once more, the owner of the 'venta' insisted on pointing out the exact spot below where the first aviators from America had touched European shore.

I was ready to see everything, and there was plenty to see. The leave-taking seminarists escorted us slowly round the Palace of the Comillas family, speaking of the old Marques with great respect and affection. I was allowed to handle the rarest books in the library, I accepted the chapel-master's invitation to try the organ with real pleasure, for its lyrical, fluting notes were much more fitting for devotional contemplation than most Spanish church organs, which, to my mind, are generally suited to emphasising the glittering drama of the world and not that of Eternity.

Then I successfully tempted the echo behind the pelota courts, while the black-gowned students interrupted their game to yodel with me. We were even given hot chocolate and a dry sponge-finger.

But the whole afternoon was tinged with melancholy and the regretful sense of irrevocable parting, as Luis and his fellows paused continually for one last look round at each familiar scene. I thought our little group of priestlings looked shrunken and forlorn as they clutched their small bundles of earthly belongings, pressed down their round beaver hats, murmured a final Adios! and clambered into the familiar old car. They spoke very little as we drove painfully and slowly down from that cool-clear atmosphere, in an evening light of amber, violet and quiet grey.

But even in this group of his contemporaries, Luis seemed to feel some personal inferiority. There was a husk of stubborn, uncouth peasantry about him which no training had polished off. It seemed to be engrained deeper than in the mere pores of his skin. Yet it was Luis who was to die young, in violence, defending his village altar in the first of the bad times that were nearer at hand than anyone guessed. And it was those local singers from the mining-hills who were to strike him down and down again to the sound of their alien chanting in that rough-cast nave. Luis was one of the very few Spaniards I ever met with no enthusiasm for the piercingly beautiful melodies of these regions. In fact, his dislike of them was strangely vehement, and I wonder now if he had some unconscious presentiment of that last event in his earthly life when the sound of them was to fall on his dying ear, exulting, without pity or ruth. 'You were begotten in obstinacy' I have heard it muttered behind your back, after futile argument had made its blows and knocks against your bullet brain steelcased in dogma. But where did the obstinacy end and your loyalty begin, for where is the human soul that has some of the one without much of the other? Well, though none of us knew it, the hidden grace was there already, for was it not by the translation of what men called your 'stupidity' into the single-minded devotion and courage that you were so early gathered to God in that crop of his nameless martyrs before the storm-clouds fully broke?

As we began the climb up the Villa that evening Teresa and Luis began to quarrel angrily. 'Don Ramón', of whom I now heard for the first time, was the subject of their argument, and what they said of him aroused my interest.

'He is too dangerous to have in the house,' said Luis flatly.

'It is only for a few weeks rest. His health is much worse.'

'It is his own fault. Why did he not go to South America? He was given his chance.'

'You know how it is. He demands to earn his bread on the soil of his fathers.'

'He deserves to starve!' Luis sounded furiously enraged.

'Well, and he is reaching that stage, it seems, so be satisfied!'

'It is all pose. If his misguided conscience, as he calls it, insists that he is in the right, why doesn't he go to some foreign University where he can preach his revolutionary gospel and atheism?'

'Because he says it is needed here more than anywhere else.'

'He will never get his Chair back in Spain, so what's the use? Teresa, think of yourself. Think of the family.'

'What else am I thinking of? He is one of yours, is he not?'

'I disowned him long ago, and you know it.'

'Well, it is no use to argue with me. He has already arrived. Look!' Luis looked and then quickly crossed himself.

'Well, I suppose you will take up your argument where you left off last year. I don't know why you always begin, since you always lose, Luis' ended Teresa, in her usual grim way, unwinding her shawl.

I watched don Ramón with great interest at dinner that evening. Externally he appeared so fine, so pure-bred an Arab that the law of improbability forbade me to take for granted the likelihood that such a type could have been preserved intact through the centuries complete with an Arab mind and character to match. There was a good deal about this manner to match his looks, however. The low, ceremonial obeisance with which he paused on the threshold, his washing of hands as a rite of ablution, his archaic formalistic salutation as he passed each table, these were fitting gestures for a man of such appearance. The incisive sweep of his gesticulation downwards – never upwards in the manner of optimists and fools – the droop of those eyelids, polite but excluding, with which, without a word, he was able to express that his opponent had made a blunder in dialectic unworthy of reply, and finally, I soon observed, the immobility with which he sat hour after hour, on the balcony, seeing nothing, hearing nothing, suffering – everything, all these characteristics were signs in keeping with his long, nervous frame, compressed, narrow head and high burning cheek-bones. He wore modern dress with a flamboyant distinction, nevertheless. His clothes were excellently cut and he always wore a neat bow in his collar, which gave him an undergraduate air on the not-very-frequent occasions when he smiled. He wore tan or black and white American shoes and carried a soft English felt hat which he balanced on his knees when listening to the ladies. He seldom talked to them. It was plain to see that he was putting some constraint on his feelings and opinions while staying at the Villa Heliotrope. Considering his reputation and that he had been out of work for nearly three years, this was not surprising. Teresa told me that his wife was still in Z ... and that she supported herself and their two children by sewing and embroidery. 'Pobrecitas' she said briefly. But it was much more than this caution, due as a guest to Teresa, that at times reacted upon his nerves and produced those acute spasms of nervous irritability he could not hide. One could see the traces of a repressive strain of long duration, of a grim battle boiling in his veins, stirring up fierce gusts and tempests of feverish calenturas. There were dark tortures raging in this soul, injustice, inhumanities, intolerable burdens he could not shift, under which his reserves of spirit were sinking very low. That same evening, when we sat stirring our coffee on the balcony, the Professor addressed me with a careful courtesy that was international in its impersonality.

'It is a great handicap,' he began, turning slightly in his chair towards me, 'a great handicap to me never to have heard Shakespeare spoken by an English man or woman.' I could not help smiling at this formal use of Shakespeare's name by way of introduction. It was, of course, impeccable.

'Yes, I can understand that difficulty,' I said at once. I was, indeed, relieved to find he had made so humble a commencement with me. I did not feel my intelligence could support argument about social revolution, still less atheism and negativist theology, but, like everyone else, I thought I could comprehend Shakespeare.

Luis sat munching biscuits and seemed not to hear what was passing. He was intent on getting Felix to bring out the coffee-pot so that the might have a second cup. And then there was the sugar-bowl to be emptied and the flies to be warded off vlgorously.

'It is a great difficulty, you know,' returned don Ramón, turning his chair towards me now, and, incidentally, turning his back on Luis who was rather noisy in his drinking.

'One peculiar to your English pronunciation, if I may say so.'

He paused, and I gave my assent with a laugh.

'Certainly, an Englishman must accept that criticism from one who speaks the most phonetically correct language in Europe!'

'Thank you!' responded don Ramón, with a half bow. 'Yes! I have read and studied him, like everyone else, and like everyone else, I think I know him very well. Yet I daresay if I were to hear you casually speak a passage from any of the great speeches – I mean the best-known ones – I should scarcely recognise it. Or, well, shall I say, that if I were to begin to declaim a passage from any given play you would die of laughing at me – that is, if you even recognised my travesty of the original.'

'Well, suppose you try,' I said, with little attempt at cunning. But he was not to be drawn.

'Oh no! Do not forget the *amor propio* of a Spaniard forbids him to place himself in anything that might resemble a ridiculous light.' I laughed, and thought of Isabel, remembering her argument. 'But I am serious! That is why a Spaniard never learns, he is so anxious always to conceal his ignorance. What barbarians we are!' Upon this I answered quickly. 'Surely the pride which conceals its ignorance is no worse than the conceit which is always trying to prove its superiority? It is less boring, at least and therefore less anti-social!'

'Ah! Do you offer that in exchange as an opposite English failing?'

'No, but I would offer the climate from which our peculiar faults proceed in exchange for the climate which produces yours.'

'I am disappointed! You have come only in search of climate?'

'Not entirely! I have come in search of myself, or so I begin to suspect.'

'Ah! And have you found anything yet? I suppose it is early days!'

'Yes and no!' I smiled back. 'Symptoms, at least – and symptoms foretell a change, you will agree!'

'I would like to ask more, but international politeness forbids.'

'I will tell you of one, because perhaps you could explain the reason of it to me. I find that whereas in England I read only prose, here in Spain I read only poetry. I am sure that means something.'

'Yes, it does. Scientists would of course say it was a demonstration of the intensifying of your metabolism, or some such thing.'

'Well, that is possibly not a bad explanation.'

'It suggests that you have already exchanged your climate for ours! I hear that you sang English songs to the children. Are there any Shakespeare examples among them, by any chance?'

'Yes, several! The cuckoo song is the one they liked best. They sing the cuckoo part and echo, you see.'

'The cuckoo song? Now, let me see. Don't tell me! The Merry Wives? No! Ah! I have it! Love's Labour's Lost.'

'Excellent!' I said promptly, with delight. 'You really know our Shakespeare, then!' Don Ramón flushed very slightly behind his ears. I had paid him the pink of compliments, in my naive way.

'That was correct? You comprehend me?'

'You mean the pronunciation? But of course!'

'Ah!' He sighed with relief and satisfaction. It seemed appropriate that Spanish *amor propio* should be more concerned with the correctness of pronunciation than with the understanding.

Luis then attempted to push himself into the conversation and Don Ramón put down his cup and saucer with a determined rattle and stood up.

'I will go down and see if there is still the same tertulia at the Café Liberal, Teresa, if you will excuse me,' he said politely.

I watched him throw the folds of an old cloak about his shoulders, a type of hooded cape I had never seen before. He saw my look of curiosity and smiled.

'This is a typical student's cloak of the nineteenth century,' he exclaimed. 'Everyone used to wear this sort of thing in my time, though they are not so common now. Soon, they will disappear entirely, which will seem incredible to my generation. Well! It was a needful friend! Only a charcoal brazier to warm one's bones by, then! The students are a pampered lot now, with their *calefacción central* and hot water to shave with! In my time I doubt if the average student was one degree more comfortable than the student of Salamanca four hundred years ago. And none the worse for it! No doubt wretchedness is a sharp spur to mental activity, though you might say we over-heated our brains by way of compensation for the draughty coldness of our attics. This modern demand for comfort above all things has broken more vital links with tradition than anything else! It never occurred to my generation that one must be at ease in order to think! The originality has gone and it is because of luxury they demand as a right. With what result? In twenty years not one student has ever surprised me with a novel thought. Think of it! Not one!'

'Yes, I put it all down to the craze for comfort nowadays and those games they play – with balls. Games with balls! Comfort and games, señorita! The English contribution to civilisation, I believe? You have a lot to answer for! So I shall therefore not invite your defence!'

'I won't attempt to argue for our love of ease, Professor, but I think our defence of games is the sublimating effect they are supposed to have on our combative instincts.'

'We should preserve our combative instincts intact for the evils and wrongs men still have to fight. You don't really believe man has ever yet achieved civilisation, do you? Good night!' And with this curt rejoinder don Ramón strode down to the town to spend the rest of the evening in the gilt-mirrored and red-upholstered Liberal Café in the arcaded Plaza Mayor.

'So you have an antipathy to comfort and games, have you?' I thought as I watched him go. And I wondered how many generations of orthodox Mohammedan ancestors and what strict sect in Arabia had caused that instinctive repulse to rise up in him in this age.

Don Ramón was regarded by the Dictatorship as too extreme a champion of intellectual toleration, but he could be very intolerant in his own personal relationships. He made no attempt to disguise his contempt for Luis' stupidity. Luis, on the other hand, was drawn by mistrust and suspicion to probe and pry where a more experienced man would have let well alone. He was obsessed by the professor's reputation and the subversive influence he was said to hold over a younger generation.

For some days, however, he let don Ramón have his own way while the Professor relaxed something of this tension, though he never bathed and seldom sat on the beach, like the other visitors. He would see him in the distance, walking slowly with his head thrust down, oblivious of a world that played about him. One night the distant thunder was so threatening that even he broke his fixed habit of visiting the Café and so found himself confronted by Luis after dinner, without hope of escape. Luis' first words showed that since their last conversation he had been incessantly turning over in his mind the same matter on which they had previously disagreed

'But tell me now, as I was trying to ask you before, what are you doing?

'Nothing.'

'Oh, come now! A man of your mental activity is always doing something! You are never idle, even in sleep, I feel sure.'

'When next I dream, Luis I will come to you for divination!'

'Come, come! I assure you I have no intention of prying into your private dream-world! Well, then, what are you *going* to do?'

'What they will let me do; you know how much that is!'

·'I know no more than you, Luis.'

'Well, well! But have you *tried* hard enough to find out what they will permit you to do?'

'I have been trying for more than two years. There is nothing. I am debarred everywhere!'

'But your wife? And the children?'

'Ah!' The Professor folded his arms over his chest. He was narrowly built. 'Teresa! I would like another coffee if I may be allowed.'

'You should consider your state of nerves,' said Luis, who pursed up his thick, pale lips and shook his head ponderously. 'Too much coffee is bad for you. You really should consider your nerves.'

'No one else does, that's plain!' Don Ramón spoke quickly with the sharp rattle of a machine-gun. Luis picked up a biscuit and broke it clumsily.

'You must exercise patience; that is all,' Luis exhorted, gulping the sweet crumbs noisily and brushing down his pleated skirts.

'I have exercised my patience so long that it is now in danger of running away with me,' was the grim retort. Don Ramón shut his eyes. He looked fatigued with despairing boredom.

'Ah, well! Ah, well! We are all in God's hands.' Luis lunged at a fly that had been troubling his nostrils. He caught and carefully stunned it, before delivering the final blow. 'Observe, don Ramón! One should always stun the *bicho* first!"

Don Ramón started slightly, then after a long stare, decided that Luis was incapable of so subtle a double meaning. If Luis had the sense to stop at this, he might have come off with the advantage of having something hidden in his hand, a trick as yet unplayed. But he could not forbear to exult in his knowledge.

'Are you trying to tell me that you have given up all thought of writing, don Ramón?'

'I am trying to talk as little as possible.'

'I can understand that!' Luis sounded as if he too, were going to try the ironic manner.

'Can you? It scarcely appears so.'

Luis began to look annoyed and the ironic pose slipped away from him. He would lose his advantage if he were not more careful.

'But in spite of what you say and in spite of what you try *not* to say, I am told you are writing still, Professor.'

'Oh, indeed! You are told I am writing! Is that so? That is very interesting news to me.' Don Ramón closed his eyes to a slit, then shot an arrow through them, straight at Luis. 'And did Socorro tell you what I was writing, don Luis?'

'How could she? The girl can neither read nor write.'

'What a pity! What a pity she cannot read my letters to my wife and children.'

'She says they cannot all be letters to your wife in such abundance.'

'Socorro underrates my family affection, I perceive. I hope Providence may send her as attentive a husband, if only to correct her point of view!'

'Socorro is a good girl,' said Luis, falling back on the defensive.

'Socorro is a simple girl,' don Ramón corrected him gravely. There was a slight pause. 'However, don't let that thought depress you, Luis.' As usual, the Professor was getting the better of Luis and, as usual, Luis was the last to perceive it.

'However, you may cheer yourself up,' said don Ramón briskly. 'I am writing something, all the same. Now I come to think of it, it should interest you very much, as a branch of sociological history not yet explored.'

'Indeed? But I am neither sociologist nor historian; and besides there is nothing new under the sun, nowadays!' Luis was sore and stiff in mood now.

'Except miracles, perhaps, to your way of thinking? And they, after all are as old as your religion! But this is merely a little light diversion to occupy my vacant time, quite innocent, I would assure you!'

'Tell us, do!' said Teresa, who had just stepped out, momentarily freed from her labours. Doña Nana, for one, would be glad of a little diversion.'

'Well, it began as an idle amusement, it is true, but I must admit that in spite of myself it is growing quite a serious affair, I give you my word. I seem to be incapable of the light touch, now that I stand in need of it. Perhaps that is a punishment for despising it at a time when I might possibly have achieved it.' His voice became gloomy at the speculation.

'But do go on,' I said, persuasively.

'It is not a lively theme, though it has its lighter moments, quite unexpectedly.'

'Yes?' We all waited. Then, abruptly, he took the plunge.

'Well, then, since you are genuinely curious to know, I am making an enquiry into the effect upon civilisation of the growing change in our disposal of the dead from earth-burial to cremation.'

'Ach!' spluttered Luis, sick with a queer, sudden disgust, spitting right out over the heliotrope bushes. Don Ramón drew away his chair. He was more nice in his manners than Luis, in spite of his Moorish appearance.

'From earth-burial to cremation!' echoed Teresa, in surprise leaning her hands over the balcony upon her right hand. 'But is there any effect? After all, the dead are dead, one supposes, in so far as the body is concerned ...'

'There is an effect upon the imagination, if that is what you mean, Teresa, and it is an influence on the minds of the living, although the dead are dead as you rightly suppose! You know as well as I do there is no such thing as a purely imaginary cause or effect, as you know that imaginative influences are never – shall we say in a narrow sense, – merely imaginary?'

'I don't know any such thing,' she retorted. 'But go on! Don't mind us and our *unacademical* ways of speaking!'

'It is a new point of view and that is what one is always looking for; a useful aspect. It enables one to put the past and present into a new and particular focus, and that is a modern historian's constant aim.'

We waited, expectantly, and surprisingly he went on. Probably he felt the lack of his old auditors and was relieved to speak his mind.

'I was not looking for a new point of view, but merely trying to fill one of many idle hours ... You now, I had been fool enough to keep my own library in the University, so that the students might use it also, and, of course, my books were confiscated entirely ... Well! Yes, as I was saying, my idle speculation has yielded some curious results, all the same. Indeed, I am not sure I have not stumbled on a factor of real potency in human energy.' He seemed to contemplate his results with warming satisfaction.

'Cremation will never be allowed in this country!' exclaimed Luis. 'Never! It is unnatural, for one thing. We are in God's hands, here!'

'Cremation is increasing in England, I believe?' don Ramón ignored Luis and suddenly shot this question at me.

'Oh, yes, rapidly! But then, we are overcrowded for space.'

'Yes! The dead threaten to exceed their natural limitations! So it begins with expediency – like all powerful forces for change – and ends with – who can say? Have you noticed any change taking place in English life in consequence?' I felt bound to take his fantastic enquiry seriously, though I could not judge whether these were the morbid fancies of a man sick with the enforced impotence of undeniably original and restless faculties. But his theory could only have evolved in a mind cut off from the living current of ideas, prematurely facing the decay of its powers and condemned by the malice of his fellow countrymen to public humiliation and private shame. I knew, too, that the town to which he had been sent under supervision was one of those provincial centres of Castile in which a certain stagnation of intellectual atmosphere bred very easily some such unhealthy miasmas as the Professor appeared to be developing. I was searching for some non-committal reply, when he bluntly put me in my place, however. 'But why do I ask you? You are too young. How can you tell? Besides, I am collecting facts at this stage, not opinions! But it is not so absurd as I suspect you think!' he said, with a grim smile. 'Examine the various civilisations of the past by their methods of burial, examine the Greeks, Homer's sense of honour, for instance, and the way of life that derived from it, by the light of their funereal pyres. Search the Roman mind by the torch-lit shadows of their tombs. You will be surprised by the unarticulated thoughts that lurk there! Then compare these with the Gothic grotesque from the North, which has made Europe for better or worse – for worse, I say! – a graveyard of our brighter urges and the clean, purged classical conception of ideas, by the perpetual contemplation of the same slow wormy path to death and dissolution. You may not agree with me, but I find your Elizabethans were rotten with it – those playwrights passed the charnel-house on their way to the theatres of Southwark and the Globe; not even Shakespeare could shake himself free of the sight. But even if you dismiss my signpost as the gibbet of a madman on the crossroads, yet as a student of literature, you must admit that the change of poetic imagery is something, as I have hinted.'

'Why, yes, that would be a great deal, especially if one believes that poets shape the world. But what? Where?'

'Examine the New World! Compare the North with the South. Yes!

'Well, examine what the North Americans are doing with the imagery, prose and poetic, how caustic and aseptic it is growing – in the land where cremation flourishes. Compare that significant improvement with the imagery of South American language. What do you find?

Mere embalming exercises in verse as in burial practices in the method prescribed by our own ancient practitioners – nothing but a cult of the dead, skull, crossbones and all, that is our Spanish gift to civilisation.'

'It would be as well if you were to leave Spain out of your consideration, if that is what you are hinting at,' said Luis with open dislike and truculence now. 'It might be dangerous for you, you know. Who can tell where it might lead to? There are many who would take very strong exception to such ideas being spread about!' Luis seemed very sure of this. He, at any rate, was not disposed to humour the Professor, as we were.

Don Ramón looked at me, at Teresa, and, last of all, at our battling priest. Then with a little smile and a bow he said: 'We are in God's hands here, as you reminded us a moment ago.' Luis looked uncertain how to take this. It sounded too orthodox to be true, coming from such a source.

'And do you think it will prove a good thing, in the long run?' I found myself asking, and almost instantaneously recognised myself as asking a typically English question in a typically English voice. Had I made such a break with my old life and come all this way only to realise that I was English after all?

'Who of us will live to see that?' he replied, turning eyes upon me that now seemed alienated, empty of interest or recognition of life, then went on: 'It may be possible that with the removal of the horrors of slow dissolution you may also remove a *wholesomely* individual fear of death and consequently of the individual sense of responsibility for the sanctity of individual human life. But man is ruthless in self-interest in every age and every climate and nothing will ever change that, I fear. That is all I can tell you, as a historian. At any rate, what I have suggested is a new line for measuring human behaviour, by our morbid fears, not of death the inevitable, but of slow decay, which is not, and since man is his own worst enemy, destroying his best potentiality and highest achievement, no new means of investigating the shadowy causes of his irrational conduct should be neglected, you will probably agree,' he ended quietly, as though folding up the sheets of a given University lecture whose conclusions he left us to ponder over.

Then an unexpected voice broke in upon our moment's thoughtfulness.

'You speak of death as if it were extinction,' said Teresa, pointedly. I had never heard her enter into argument before.

'It is the extinction of what we know,' he reminded her, gravely.

'And the beginning of what we believe,' Luis almost shouted at him, astonished to hear himself deliver an affirmation of faith in so prompt a manner. He gulped in a new air of superiority. But not for long.

'Is that why the contemplation of dissolution stimulates the imaginative appetite, can you tell me, then?' the Professor demanded roughly.

'Why ask me? That is not my province,' said Luis with dignity which was stiffening into the old dogma.

'Is it not? What of your mystics, pray?'

'Sir?' countered Luis, crouching mentally, like an animal uncertain whether his enemy is attempting a trap to ensnare him.

'Well,' the Professor said, impatiently, 'we won't waste our time on that.' This drew Luis on, of course.

'I suppose you were going to bring up the case of Santa Teresa again?'

'I was. I was. But it is quite unimportant, when all's said and done.' Don Ramón could be quite diabolical in his irritation. Luis knew that of old, plainly. I recalled that Isabel had once said in my ear 'Teresa is the only woman men really argue about. I wonder why?'

'You are the Devil's Advocate of our age, I suspect, señor,' Luis was accusing don Ramón, now. 'But let me tell you, you are caught in the toils of your own cleverness when you dare to tread upon that ground. For when you throw out your insinuations about Santa Teresa you reveal the true source of your thoughts. When you mention that, you tell me the books you have read – and also, and more significant, the books you have not read.'

'And never shall. And never shall!' cried don Ramón with a sweep and cutting downward gesture of his hands that relegated Luis and all his authorities to the limbo of the chrysom child.

'You are a danger to the peace of the world,' flamed Luis. 'There is a taint upon your soul that nothing can save! You lay an obscene hand of doubt on all that has been proved sacred to man In his weakness. But beware of the day of your own need. What will save you then? You will send for me at the last! And doubtless you will expect me to come. I know your kind.'

Don Ramón had picked up his hat and was about to go down the steps. He turned. 'And you – you would come?' he asked with mockery.

'It's not fair' Teresa murmured in my ear. 'Luis is only an inexperienced boy!'

Luis was goaded beyond ordinary endurance. He essayed to speak, and the struggle shook his frame. Aid came from an unexpected quarter and from a woman.

'I have stood on this balcony for fifteen years,' said Teresa, 'listening to men talk, talk, talking about life and death, proving with every other word that they know nothing about either. Why will you always choose subjects about which you are so ignorant? Because you can go on and on endlessly, I suppose. You have no sense! Why can't you be like us, to have the wisdom to speak about the things we know, and things we know only?'

'Because' said don Ramón, in equally ironic tones, 'there would be really nothing to argue about!'

'So much the better! So much the better!' retorted Teresa with scorn. 'If it makes for less talk, and more work! But I will tell you one thing, don Ramón. Until you find means to bind the dead, you will never lead the living, which is what you long to do like the rest of your kind.'

'I will do what I have to do for the living, Teresa, and for the future that is yet to come. They would not leave me to do my work as the historian I was made to be. In humanity's name then I will prove to them than one act of free will, here and now, is more vital to the march of man in progress even than tearing off the bandage from that running sore they dignify by calling history! Let Luis there perform the rites of expiation to the past that is gone. Let him propitiate the spirits of revenge and sin. I have no time for the dead – at present!'

'How do you know what is living and what is dead?' said Teresa, harsh and vehement as she stood above him on the steps. 'By your nose, I suppose? That is your modem way!'

'The nose is a useful organ, Teresa. And none the less useful for being a humble creature, nor so easily deceived as the eye and ear, because it is not so easily flattered. You are quite right there.'

'Bah! Nor am I so easily deceived by flattery from you, don Ramón!' Then she went on. 'And I will tell you another thing, don Ramón. There are many dead with more power than the living, and millions living with less power than one dead man or woman.'

'If you are thinking in terms of power ...'

'It is all you men ever think about, believe me,' said Teresa and withdrew to the door into the house.

The Professor looked at us and shrugged his shoulders. 'You see what we have to contend with in this country?' he said to me. 'The women are the ebb-tide of our civilisation in Spain,' he added.

'If that is so, don Ramón,' said Teresa distinctly, 'it is because men reserve their habits of acquired civilisation for their relations with other men and the indulgence of their savageries for the part of their lives they share with women.' She folded her arms over her breasts as she spoke, but though she appeared quite calm there was a more deeply resonant tone in her voice than usual. He looked back at us from the foot of the steps, seemed as if about to speak, but shrugged his shoulders instead and made us one of those sweeping gestures of sceptic negativism which were one of the most positive expressions of his nature.

'He will have to leave before the royal visitors arrive,' fumed Luis after he had disappeared, pursing up his thick pale lips, 'or there will be a scandal! It's in his nature, I do believe, not even a knife could cut it out of him. He has an instinct to handle dangerous matters. In fact, everything he touches turns to sedition or blasphemy, usually both, usually both!'

'He is an original man,' said Teresa. 'We have very few left. It is a cruel shame!'

'You mean he is an arrogant man,' retorted Luis. 'Why can't he be content with a simple view of life? He complicates things quite need-lessly. I'd like to know what he is doing here just now!'

'He is here for his health,' said Teresa very quickly. 'Anyone can see how ill he is, and you may be sure he will take himself off to suit what he finds to be my convenience, when the visitors arrive. They are not his sort. He no more wants to see them, than they wish to see him!'

'Teresa, you should be more careful! It will make a scandal, mark my warning! I don't know what's taken you this summer. There are all sorts of strange things going on in the mountains between here and the frontier and it behoves us all to be very careful. People making their way out and others slipping in. Nobody knows where it will end, and that's the truth.'

'It will never end!' said Teresa with more weariness in her voice than usual.

'It is true what Isabel said,' I ventured. 'In Spain in the depth of soil is too shallow. It cannot hold the water, even on those rare days when the rain falls abundantly. And underneath is the rock that men can never move. You must plant trees again, to bind the earth as she said. That is all.'

'The prosperous are too egotistical and the poor too wretched to have patience to think for the future,' was all Teresa said, as we went in.

'So that is the metal of which these Castilians are made' I said to myself as I went to bed that night. 'A hard inflexible metal, beaten and hammered upon by white-hot passion, sudden fire as suddenly quenched in the ice-cold water of reality. And then it is sharpened to a sword's-edge by the endurance of keen winds in high desolate places.'

Once more I looked out into the night across the mountains over this country where there was great silence but no peace.

The Two Nuns of Barcelona

WHEN I DECIDED TO GO up to Barcelona that April I should have guessed that there would probably be trouble. The autumn riots in Madrid, the shootings in the streets, the night patrols passing incessantly about the suburbs – more then once I myself had been stopped and questioned on my way home from the *zarzuela* theatres I frequented down beyond the Puerta del Sol – the flight of that air squadron from the barracks of Cuatro Caminos over the Royal Palace where it swooped menacingly low to drop its showers of threatening pamphlets – the unhappy, heavy face of the Queen when she made one of her rare appearances in public, all these portended a troubled time. Even in Málaga, to which I had made my way in the New Year, there were disturbances; the night I went to the wooden, cheap little theatre on the *muelle*, hoping to see some performance salted with the wit of the local sailors and fishermen for whom it catered, it was rushed by the police and the audience was asked to leave. An old church in the narrow lane was burned on the next Sunday night, and so the signals of unrest flickered up and down the country.

But it was on a tranquil sunset evening that I set foot on the tiny Basque cargo boat in Málaga harbour. The pale stone walls and towers of the cathedral warmed to the tinge of human flesh as the hot sun dipped below the sea, and when I had placed my baggage in the little cabin assigned to me next to that of the captain's wife, and had come on deck again, the cathedral bell was tolling out the hour of nine. It was dark now and we turned about and were soon at sea. Our little coaster chugged along quite unconcernedly. Always it kept quite close in to shore, so that as the moon rose I could discern the coastline – low – sparsely dotted with palm-trees, solitary or in groves. The moon deepened to coppery tones in the warm, dense air and the night was so still that once or twice I thought I could hear the ripples made on the surface of the water by the flying fish as they leaped, gaping, so it seemed, to see us pass so silently along those fabled shoals.

It is the habit of these little boats to sail by night and unload by day; and excellent way of life to the ruminative traveller. I did not trouble to go ashore. Why should I? The ship's cook prepared wholesome, simple dishes and it was much pleasanter to doze by day among a haze of masts and sails and listen to the rising and lowering of cranes, the crank of wheels, the creak of timber, than to wander through the glaring dockland streets of towns I already knew well enough. The proper time to come fully awake was after sundown when the wind freshened and we put out to sea again and the coils of rope on the deck made convenient nests from which to watch the gliding scene of Mediterranean quiescence.

Almeria, Cartagena, Alicante, Valencia, Tarragona, Altos Hornos; in a week we approached, entered and left behind all these. I did not bother to buy newspapers. Where was the need? They obscured the truth, anyway. So when at length we dropped anchor somewhere below the Montjuich barracks in Barcelona docks, I sauntered ashore as though the times were normal enough and my own life as detached from passing events as ever.

My lodging had been arranged and I was expected by my Murcian host and his wife. They had an apartment on the third floor of a large block of flats on the outskirts of Barcelona on the way towards the popular Sunday resort of pine-woods at Las Planas. There was no made-up road for the last half-mile of the track and odd cabbage plots and bean-fields got in the way of the other houses and cabins round about. The only visible paving was that in front of the newly-built church across the sand-pit from where don Felipe and his wife, Esmeralda, lived. Don Felipe's sister, whom I knew, was reasonably comfortably off, but I soon found out that her brother was glad to receive even the modest sum I was prepared to pay for my board and lodging. Although a steady-earner as accountant in a Barcelona joint stock bank, he had developed a costly and unfortunate hobby; a feud with a government department. He was one of that numerous Murcian colony resident in Catalonia, and should, by his industry and modest style of living, have had a reasonable chance of living happily ever after, like others from his province who had found employment in the more prosperous parts of Catalonia. But no! He had had the ill-luck to inherit a small piece of land in Murcia – derelict except for a few almond-trees beneath which the Moors were traditionally supposed to have once worked a silver mine. On a fateful holiday he had had the curiosity to explore the closed-up gallery on his estate with a Catalan-like spurt of energy and had had the still greater ill-fortune to discover an infinitesimal thread of silver; it could not be called a vein, so doña Esmeralda privately explained to me. Excited beyond reason, fevered past coherent dreaming, he had become a demented man – except when in his office, adding up his columns, for he was a conscientious, meticulous man in everything else that did not concern his silver-mine – resolved at all costs to exploit the hidden treasure he was certain lay beneath his feet, incontestably, by the law of inheritance, his! But alas! a Government permit was necessary before he could begin to clear out the choked-up debris of centuries – and no Government official could be found to grant him one. He carried his obsession and the handful of pernicious silver evidence from department to department. The fever had become a conviction and he was now that most unhappy of creatures, a man with *ineradicable* grievance.

His wife said little about her share of this burden, but I gathered that her dote had vanished in the expense of his going to Madrid with a vague and involved plan of circumventing a Barcelona high official by interviewing a higher one there and so on. The couple had one little boy, born in the first year of their marriage, but since the discovery of the Moorish mine the family had not increased.

Within a few days I was settled down into my usual musical habits and it was a bright spring morning – Sunday – when I made my way into a theatre on the Paralelo at about ten, forty-five o'clock. A green-coloured bill had been thrust into my hands on the evening before when I was strolling down the Ramblas admiring the flowerstalls and listening to the full-whistling chirping of the famous sparrows. This announcement of a Grand Festival of the Sardana, an event to be cel-ebrated by the participation of a band of musicians and dancers from Valencia and Tarragona, roused my curiosity. Evidently, it was to be no ordinary festival that brought a hundred men all that distance to spend Sunday in Barcelona. And so thought the police and military authorities, I quickly noticed, as I pushed my way into the back rows of the pit-stalls. I was slow to see what was plain to everyone else. This was an organised act of defiance – a political demonstration for which music was an obvious pretence. The huge stage was crammed with dock-workers solidly grouped behind their banners – syndical-ists, socialists, anarchists. And in the aisles, guarding the exits – ah! I was beginning to learn with what light heart one could make an entrance into such places in Spain and with what growing anxiety one would look furtively back for possible exits! – were double files of armed police and those long-suffering, most mildly domesticated of men, in private life, the Guardia Civil.

The music proceeded with reasonable adherence to the programme for about twenty-minutes, though the cheers, stampings and calls from the audience showed some impatience with this pretence. I could not understand most of the remarks that rang out challenging-ly in Catalan, but the temper of the theatre began unmistakably to rise. Well! We should see now! Having shown what each group could accomplish separately, the banners and their upholders now con-verged and combined and after a deliberate silence their instruments struck up the *toque* or call, to a sardana. Here they stopped again, and there was an expectant hush. Then someone called out from the stage and pointed towards a box on the ground level. There were cheers and cheers again and a black-suited figure rose from his seat and bowed. Maestro Morera! Maestro Morera! The shout went up, and the composer of the forbidden Catalan Sardana, La Santa Espina, rose politely again. Ah! We all knew to expect now! Even I knew what I should hear next – though it was not named on the pro-gramme. The bands prepared to sound their call to freedom. But such a great roar went up that I barely heard the first two bars, let alone the opening phrase in its entirety. The cheering and stamping burst forth again. Again the musicians struck up and again the music was drowned in the tumult. The house rose deliriously. The police made no disguise of their cordon now. But again the music threw down the gage of defiance before them. And again the crowd roared. They needed no conductor; their hearts and souls were in this business. Eleven times La Santa Espina struggled to be heard before that audi-ence calmed sufficiently to allow it to be played, and they calmed their enthusiasm only in order to sing in unison. Their unanimity was fervent; almost I should have called it ferocious, had I not looked about me and seen the glistening eyes of honest-seeming men, recall-ing acts of repression and injustice of which I had never heard.

The curtains at the back of the stage moved suddenly and the per-formers were surrounded. No one was arrested, but the hint was taken. The musicians put down their instruments, the singers with their banners filed off; and after a moment's uncertainty, the audience, too, decided to disperse; it was a comparatively peaceful occasion, dissolving in uncertainty. But it was to prove the last.

A day or two later I began to see that the air was full of strained expectancy. When I went to a newspaper stall near the University I was surprised to see workmen buying and openly carrying away coloured prints of Captain Galán's photograph. Galán! The soldier who had been shot for leading the recent abortive rising of the Jaca garrison! I watched an elderly worker in a blue smock carefully put his change in a wallet and then gaze earnestly at the photograph and walk away proudly with his purchase. I looked round. There were no police to be seen anywhere. That night there was a red glare in the sky – a church was being burned. The nuns were going into hiding, it was whispered.

Two days later and there was a sense of holiday about the city though it was mid-week and no great saint's day. As I walked towards the main avenue – the exercise was good for the voice, and I often walked the whole distance to my singing lesson – I noticed workmen in clean smocks and overalls, cleanly shaven and spruced, walking in small groups toward the town. It seemed like a fair day. Everyone was good-humoured and a good deal of quiet chaffing went on, though this seemed to die down as we converged on the Paseo de Gracia. Usually, I turned off to the left at Calle Aragón, but his morning I played truant and with my music tucked under my arm I followed the growing crowd down towards the great Plaza de Catalunya. Well, as I was growing to know, it was easy to get into a place but difficult to get out of it again. The crowd was so dense in the Plaza that I suddenly tried to get away towards the British Club in Fontanella, where it then was. But it was impossible now to make any further individual decision. I was carried along, squeezed to one side till I found myself stranded at the corner where the Plaza is reached by the main Rambla coming up from the docks and the harbour, on the right. I suddenly realised why I had seen so few police and soldiery about so far. They were all concentrated here or hereabouts. The mounted police were out in force this morning – and as if there were not already enough of them, the familiar jingle and trot of cavalry suddenly broke out from the roads debouching on the Plaza from the barracks of Montjuich. We civilians were so many now we could not escape being downtrodden by the horses, it seemed, and if it pleased their commanders to give the word, we should be mown down silently like grass. Alarmed at my position in that exposed, strategic spot, I looked quickly round, decided to run for shelter immediately, whatever the cost to my pride, and to my horror saw that the neighbouring shopkeepers had also decided that it was the moment to take cover and that they were closing down their doors. I made one last effort to reach the shelter of a silversmith's entrance, but the assistant, who was standing with the long-arm rod in his hands, suddenly crashed down the steel shutters before my face and darting behind the aperture banged that finally behind him. Well, had to face the music now, whatever it might be! Would it be hiss of bullets – the bugle-call to charge, or the stuttering recitativo of the machine-gun? I had heard them all at a distance – elsewhere – but I had never been within more than two streets of the actual reality, except for one or two casual bombs several hundred feet or yards behind my back, and there had always been a cellar handy or a friendly corner close by to run to. As I could not get away, I began to look at the people round me with intent interest. In other parts of Spain they told queer stories of the Catalan quick temper. But I found I dreaded most of all the nervous starts and fidgets of the cavalry chargers as they edged us now on and now off the pavement into the gutters. Their riders seemed to be chewing their chin-straps more than usual, I noticed. What were they waiting for? What were we all waiting for?

A low sound as of the sea began to rise like a tide far down the Ramblas. What were they doing down there in the docks and arsenals? And what was the instinct that had drawn all Barcelona towards this historic spot this morning of an April mid-week?

We had not long to wait, now. The low sound rose and swelled into a roar. Looking down beneath the lines of trees, I saw banners bobbing up and down, coming nearer, steadily rising with the march of thousands of firm-footed Catalan working men. The roar grew deafening though it was still indistinct. Above it, to our right, the sharp order of one voice, cut across our wondering speculation, and made us aware of our imminent danger caught between opposing forces that in a moment would confront each other. The cavalry, the Guardia Civil and the armed police closed in round the square, then turned and faced the rising rhythm of the workers on the march. If battle were to be given, it must be here and now. My legs were giving way beneath me. I had had space to fall, I should have fallen then and there. We could see the guns and swords in the Plaza. But what arms did this unknown challenge carry? Bombs we might expect, but how many and how powerful?

Then, to my surprise, under the very noses of the cavalry, in the front line of their range of fire, the peaceful civilians all round me suddenly drew forth forbidden emblems, republican colours. They were tying them round one another's arms, they were sticking provocative *mottos* on their caps, in their buttonholes. Then, after this brisk little local scuffle, as it were, there was a sudden stillness and heads were lifted keenly, awaiting yet another command. It came. The same, sharp, high voice of armed authority. The mob had reached the limit of the Rambla. Another pace forward and they would swing and surge into the Plaza. They halted and there was a moment of dead silence. We all knew what the consequence of one more step would be.

And then – oh, from whence did it come? – we felt a breath of genius – a touch of the miraculous that stirred in the air and leaped across the antagonist gulf by which we were divided. The day of Saint George was nearly upon us. It seemed to some of us in that moment that he took time by the forelock and came to save his Catalan protégés from mutual self-destruction that morning. An unknown man, leaped suddenly out from behind us, and with the genial lightning improvisation for which the Catalan people are known, tore the streamer from the shoulders of the dockland leader in the front and quicker than thought, quicker than the colonel's next word of command, thrust it round the neck of the foremost sergeant of the guard as he was bending forward to loose his sword for the charge.

'You are OUR soldiers now,' this unknown genius cried. 'You are OUR soldiers now!'

And the sergeant laughed, as he found his arm entangled in the ribbons. He could not stop himself. The tension had been grim. The Catalans took their cue from their unknown spokesman. 'You are our army now' they cried, and there was a rush forward with armlets, bands and streamers. In a moment, the soldiers, even the Guardia Civil, were garlanded and festooned with Republican tri-colours. The relaxation was immediate. Faces lit up as it was seen that the soldiers halted uncertainly, reluctant to move. Some were seen to smile sheepishly, slowly. Clearly, their hearts had not been in this business. Then a great laugh went up. Slowly, like a great bubble it lifted and drifted back and forwards from one side to another – from civilians to soldiery – and then, last of all, it burst with a roar of a splitting blast from the mob stationed at the head of the Ramblas. The merriment became gigantic. Danger and death had been very near. But its very nearness had been our saving.

They had seen each other face to face, they had sensed each other's mood and felt our common human need.

All that day, the Catalan people rode about on their municipal trams, waving flags, singing, singing La Santa Espina and Els Segadors, – the old song of The Reapers – with which the morning's crucial moments had melted into common day. Up and down they went, up and down, endlessly, nobody paying, nobody asking for payment. This was their first free day. The people's first, free day. Then came the certain news that Alfonso had fled. 'I will have no blood shed' were his last words on Spanish soil, so we heard. There was a momentary cloud of thoughtfulness at this. But then, as we all laughed and said, 'Ah! but the Catalans thought of that first!' and out burst the singing again and up and down they rode again in their trams, and taxis, too, so it had come about by this time in the evening.

All the same, I was glad to stay near at home for a few days. I had had a great fright, and I hopefully thought I had learned the value of prudence.

There were great comings and goings. Openings of prisons, chiefly; not much thought of vengeance in those first days. Nobody seemed to think of that. Freedom! Freedom! That was the thought in everyone's mind. So the prisons emptied and the wrongfully persecuted came forth to take the places of honour in government and some of the justly sentenced managed to get out into the daylight, too.

Then the Catalans announced the setting up of their autonomous state and mutterings began. The Castilians would not like that! Extremist voices began to sound a shrill note and slogans that were not as yet to be voiced in the council chamber were chalked boldly across the roads and upon the walls. There were explosions again at night; we had thought that with the Republican success such things had become nightmares of the past. And again there were red glares to betoken the burning of churches. Quiet, comfortable and modest-living people like don Felipe and his wife began to look uneasy and preoccupied.

One morning she announced that they were expecting two cousins from the country on a visit. She thought we should not be unduly cramped by their presence. In any case they were shy and retiring, unaccustomed to meeting strangers, and they would not be in my way. She added as an afterthought, that of course they would only be in Barcelona for a few days at the most.

I soon discovered that the pair of country cousins not only kept out of my way but out of everyone else's, so far as that was possible. They shared the room next to mine. We were on the inner side of the block of apartments, looking out on to the patio which served as a private retreat for the other tenants also. But before her relatives arrived doña Esmeralda had marked off their share of the balcony from mine by a tolerably thick screen of oleander bushes, climbing geraniums and genista in tubs and pots. There was a communicating door between my room and theirs, but it had always been locked and so it remained.

Since I lunched in town and they did not supper late at the usual Barcelona hour of nine, it was a long time before I met the newcomers face to face. Now and then I heard them engaged in monotonously long and low monologues, so it sounded, till I realised that they spent regular hours in prayer, and now and then I would get a faint waft of incense rising up from under the door between us, for though it was locked, it was never sealed. They never appeared on the balcony and though I passed their door many times a day it was always closed, and for the first week I got no glimpse of them whatever. I was interested, of course, but my curiosity never overstepped the line into active inquisitiveness, so I was content to see them moving: once or twice I caught them hurrying away before me in the dark corridor we shared, and of course I was careful not to show any sign of attempting to overtake them nor even to greet them with a Good morning or Good night. I had asked doña Esmeralda to tell me their names, and she had told me that they were doña Iria and doña Eulalia respectively. She said nothing of their surnames. And I was glad she made no attempt to invent any, since she was a very poor liar and sounded as uncomfortable as I felt when my innocent questions necessitated some improvisation on her part.

Then one day I was coming down from the roof where I had been drying some things and at the turn of the stairs immediately above, I heard the two sisters talking, arguing almost, it seemed, at the top of the lift shaft, and one of them was rebuking the other. I halted just in time to hear her.

'But we were told not to use the lift on any account. You know that very well.'

'What was the harm in it, just once? There was nobody about and it is no sin. I just wanted to see what it was like. Of course I won't do it again.'

The voice was gentle, pleading. The reply was made almost as softly, but with more decision in its inflection. 'There are others to think of besides ourselves. You might bring trouble on them, by your thoughtless impulse. It was disobedience, too.'

'I have promised never to do it again. I just wanted to try it once. Besides, we shall be gone very soon now, shall we not?'

'I don't know. I don't know. We were only coming here for a week at first and now, it seems almost certain we cannot go back.'

'Well, everything is all right, you see. Nobody was about. And I will never, never do it again; though, as you saw, it was nothing at all, really, was it now?'

'Sister Eulalia,' began the other, with some firmness, then stopped. She had seen me. 'Hush! Hush!' she said in a quick whisper and immediately both of them had pressed back against the wall, obviously wishing it might open and envelop them from view. As I passed, they pressed their voluminous skirts behind them with deprecating gestures and almost hidden hands. I wanted to assure them of my friendliness and discretion, but they were so nervous that I did not dare to stop and say a word. I tried to smile at each sister, but I got no answering look in return. Both of them immediately looked down upon the ground and remained gazing so. I had read their secret and they knew that I had.

I had, however, seen enough to realise a considerable difference in their two natures. Sister Eulalia, who had longed to venture upon a forbidden lift-ride, was the elder of the two, with thinning hair that still curled a little. She was comfortably fleshed, and had she not been frightened out of her wits by the sight of me on the stairs would have seemed almost jolly and buxom, though her eyes were innocently, blankly blue. Sister Iria was altogether more remarkable. I would have liked to see that oval face framed in nun's coif; but even in secular dress and uncovered head, there was an aloofness about her carriage which I was not altogether sure to be derived from her spiritual withdrawal. But though the lines of her mouth and chin – this was surprisingly rounded – were firmly held, there was transparency of hue about her eyes whose pupils were delicately pencilled as if by a master-hand of pastel-drawing. The expression on her face of a firm will and sensitive perception combined was delightful to see, and I found my interest in the quiet movements and murmurs in that room next door touched now with genuine sympathy. For doña Eulalia's childish wonder in the changing world she had emerged upon after long seclusion, I felt an amused compassion, but not much more.

Fortunately, ours was not the only household jogged out of its usual habits by political circumstances. There were comings and goings everywhere, family conclaves, visits of friends from a distance to discuss problematical contingencies, withdrawings of children from schools at a distance, and so on, so that the visit of two country cousins, who went regularly to the church over the way every morning and evening, was scarcely remarked, and their prolonged stay almost unnoticed. Gradually, the two nuns settled down to our uneventful secular way of living and even became reconciled to meeting me momentarily about the corridors. They wore stuff and alpaca gowns, high-necked, short-waisted and full in the skirt, one navy blue, – doña Eulalia, – doña Iria in black. They wore their rosaries, of course, and when they slipped out over the way they draped little shawls closely around their shoulders and mass veiling over their heads and faces. Then one evening, there was a more pronounced dispute between the sisters which I overheard quite plainly, not because I was eavesdropping, but because their voices were sufficiently sharp to be heard through the crack in the door between us. Again it was doña Iria who was rebuking doña Eulalia, her elder. 'You should have come straight back.' 'I came very quickly. I hurried.' 'That was the surest way to bring notice upon yourself.' 'I assure you it was quite dark.' 'I know it was. It is of that I am complaining. You are very late, very late, much too late. No woman should be out in the streets alone after dark.'

'YOU were invited, too.'

'I did not accept.'

'Come! You know it was left to our discretion to take reasonable recreation.'

'Yes. It was left to our discretion – OUR discretion, not yours or mine, singly.'

'She has always been a loyal patron of our house. Everyone knows that.'

'Too many people know it.'

'She wished to help us. That was why she sent the invitation.'

'She is helping us! But we are not helping her by calling openly at her house.'

'She asked us to go.' Doña Eulalia could be quite stubborn, I perceived.

'Yes, but she would have understood had you refused. Perhaps she would have appreciated that as a delicacy.' Doña Iria also held to her point of view. 'Well, she asked us and I went. I was glad to go. We see nobody here, far less than in the convent. And there, there is always something to do.'

'We knew it would be an exercise in fortitude when we left the convent.'

'Yes, but this is an exercise in patience, and that is always the more difficult,' sighed Sister Eulalia. Sister Iria made no audible reply to this.

'She had asked my niece to be there this afternoon. Did you know that?'

'No. I did not.'

'It was very kind of her, I thought. Very kind.'

'Yes. She is well, your niece, I suppose?'

'Very well. And she brought three of the children for me to see. Imagine, they have six already, and she is only twenty-seven. He says they will have ten before they finish."

'Sister Eulalia!'

'It is only an innocent little family joke. Why, she said it before the children quite simply, and they all laughed, too. They are such happy little dears. Two of them sat on my lap at once. They asked me to merienda, next Sunday.'

'Ah!'

'They asked you, too, of course, Sister Iria. I wish you would come.'

'Do you mean you will go out again – next week?'

'I said a prayer with the children before I left – they repeated it after me. And look! They gave me this bag of sweets for you – hon-eyed figs! I have eaten nine.

'Oh, Sister Eulalia, you are too fond of such things.'

'Come now, you know we are allowed to make little sweetmeats for our saints' days.'

'You are always making them, I know.'

'I make them well, at least so everyone in the convent says. I have promised to make something for the children next Sunday.'

'You have agreed to go then? Without consulting me, or Father Sebastian?'

'I am going to read to them from my book of the saints. They are sadly backward in reading, it seems. It is such a pity. She says she has no time for it, with the babies. It is such a pity. They are really such good little children. What were you going to say?'

'Nothing. But perhaps you had better tell Father Sebastian in the morning.'

'If you think it best. Have you seen my prayer-book? Thank you. Thanks.' And there was silence till bed-time. Then I heard the blowing out of candles before each crept into her narrow iron bed.

Very soon I had cause to speculate more closely about the future of my neighbour nuns. The Generalitat – the Catalan Government – was tightening its grip on affairs, the more quickly because it was becoming increasingly plain that Madrid did not like this autonomous turn of events in Catalonia, the richest, the most progressive province of Spain. The central government saw clearly that this was the first blow at Republican unity, and a vital one, because it came from within. The Catalans were proving deaf to all persuasion. Autonomy was a century-old dream, whose realisation had appeared impossible. Now it had come true overnight. They had yet to learn the truth of the proverb 'Easy win, easy lose.'

Pageantry and poetry were the external order of the day. The cabinet's most prominent members were orators, writers and poets, returned from exile and prison, whence their emotional declarations of the sacred function of the Catalan language had been smuggled into Barcelona and printed by underground agitators. Printing presses clattered out a spate of books in Catalan; there were concerts, illuminations, unveilings of statues, processions; fountains streamed, oratory flowed over in every square. Overnight, it seemed, the Catalan people leaped into new life: mobile, voluble, ingenious, triumphant. People flocked to the parks on Sunday morning to dance the Sardana, as their ancestors had thronged the churches. I saw staid elderly men throw their hats into the ring where the children turned and sang, and make a ever widening circle about them with other respectable citizens, many of them almost past dancing, but still capable of reflecting this mood of a newly wakened power, irresistibly exhilarating.

Decrees issued so fast from the Generalitat palace that one could not keep pace with them all. There were two, however, of which I learned in the same day. They sent me home more thoughtful than usual. One decree announced the reform of the divorce laws; nearly all my acquaintances were shaking their heads and pursing up their lips about the wisdom of this extreme relaxation. The other decree proclaimed that men and women in holy orders might return to secular life if they wished.

It had been a glittering day of unabating effervescence in the city and the streets were crowded and noisy. I was glad therefore to drag out my wicker-work low chair on to the balcony outside my room and look out towards the tree tops of Las Planas in the cool of the evening. Meditating on the speed at which events in Spain were now moving and on the good fortune of my several artist friends who were all, it seemed, intoxicated by the new scope offered to them by the generous schemes of the young autonomous State, I suppose I fell into a quiet doze, because I suddenly realised with a jerk that the window of my two nuns had been opened and that candles had been lit on the little table where they kept their images. For a moment, as I watched doña Iria flitting about the room, making no sound and doña Eulalia taking off her shawl and then her coat, folding, then unfolding them over and over again in silent agitation, I thought I was still dreaming, but then they began to talk, and I confess I decided at that moment to keep quite still behind the screen of plants and shrubs. It was obvious by their restlessness that they had heard of the decree. Did they think, like some thoughtful civilian persons, that behind this apparently liberal gesture lurked a momentous foreboding to those who did not choose to take the opportunity it offered?

As if in answer to my thought, doña Iria sat down and folded her hands in her lap.

'Sister Eulalia!' she began.

'Yes?'

'Why are you so agitated?'

'Not more than usually nowadays, surely?'

'I think you are.'

'It is all so confusing.'

'Why should you find it so? Surely the decree makes no difference to you either way?'

'Does it not to you, Sister Iria?'

'None whatever! How could it ever?'

There was a moment's silence.

'Well –' began Eulalia and halted. 'But – do you think many will avail themselves of it?'

'A secular decree? I pray not. We must all pray not!' Iria spoke with energy.

'But – could one wholly blame them, do you think? I mean –' Eulalia halted again.

'I mean – when shall we be able to return to the convents, for instance?'

'Does that trouble you? Since you appear to have taken the secular announcement more to heart than perhaps you should, do not forget that the decree explicitly promises and guarantees safety and peace to all those who return to their religious houses! Or is your trust in the power of these secular authorities to enforce their promises not so complete, after all?'

'No, except that they also promise that there shall be no molestation of anyone returning to their friends or families, but that all shall live in quiet without fear!'

'Ah!' Iria's voice was quietly penetrating. 'And are you prepared to trust that promise rather than the other?'

'No – but – whose word can we take in this? If the Monarchy could not control the mobs – Heaven forgive my uncharitable expression, but you know what I mean, the unenlightened people – what are we to expect of this makeshift government, without experience, and a separatist party, into the bargain? Who can we trust?'

'Surely you know the answer to that, Sister!' Iria's voice was low and urgent. There was no moralising about the way she spoke. Her retort came with the vivid force of direct experience of life upon another plane.

'Yes. I know. We trusted our souls to Heaven on the night we left the convent. But here we are.'

'Some, I daresay, may be tempted, but only a few, I am sure – the weak, the wavering and we must try to strengthen them, not only by our prayers, but with example!' Iria's energy was admirable.

'Yes, Sister Iria. But of course, you have never been tempted.' Eulalia was quite as direct in her simple way.

'Have you, Sister Eulalia?' These religious sisters were more relentless in their searching of each other's secret thoughts than any secular women would dare to be. 'Have you, Sister Eulalia?'

'Yes. Yes. But then ...'

'Then? What?'

'Perhaps I have prayed too much for myself and not enough for the others and that is why I sin.' Eulalia sighed a little. 'But I need it more than most. Grace, I mean.'

'It is a sign of Grace to see your fault so plainly. You must not be so despondent over your own failings. It leads to weakness, you know.'

'Oh, yes, I know the handicap of seeing my sins so clearly. I only wish I could see so clearly in all the other problems of this life!'

'When we get back to our customary ways all this will seem a nightmare, a passing disorder. You will see. Only let us have patience. This will soon be over.'

'For you, yes – but not for me. No! Let me go on. After all, you have your double vocation, as it were, a dedication of your mind as well as of your spirit. Your books, your studies, the things you are beginning to write.'

'You too have your double vocation, as you call it, Sister Eulalia. You have a quick heart to support your spirit.'

'A quick heart to feel, but a slow brain to learn, too slow ever to see clearly.'

'You have been a nun for twenty-five years – ten years longer than I have – and you have always been exemplary.'

'Yes, I have been a nun for a quarter of a century and for the last ten years I have tried not to face the fact that mine is not a true vocation; that is why I have tried to make it an honest one, Sister Iria, because, in a way, I am a cheat!'

'You are not seeing clearly now. The suspense, the upheaval has frightened you a little. Everything is strange and unaccustomed. That is natural, but it will pass.'

'No, no. It is true I am a little frightened, but this will not pass. I mean this denial of my real self that I have kept secret for so long.'

'Do not say it! Do not speak words you may regret afterwards.'

'But I must. It is now or never with me. I am more frightened of continuing this cheat than of all the revolutions in the world!' Eulalia's voice trembled with despair. Iria moved swiftly near the towards her troubled sister.

'I must not let you say this. You need help, support. Remember our rule of silence when we are in doubt. Let us not speak any more to-night.'

'But I am NOT in doubt, I tell you. I am suffering the terror of certainty!' The anguish of this weak woman in the grip of overmastering self-knowledge was extreme. I drew back a little, ashamed to witness her intimate revelation.

'They have been tempting you to leave us,' said Iria, after a pause.

'They have offered me a home. I think I should have left you in any case, and God knows what would have come to me, the weak, silly creature that I am, and should be, wandering out into the world, alone. But, Sister Iria, I cannot explain it, I cannot understand it, but it seems that God is being good to me in a way that I do not deserve; at a time when so many are in trouble. He has shown me a way to find peace … a way out of doubt and torture for many years.'

'Do you mean you plan to leave us – now, when we need to stand firm?'

'Do you not see, this is the testing time – and I am not one of you, sister?'

'You prefer the uncertain charity of men to the Eternal Love of Jesus, Eulalia?'

'They need me.'

'They never felt the need before you visited their home. You have no money. You would be the unpaid drudge – the servant of all the household.'

'Perhaps. But there are all those children to love and teach. And his mother. You know she is bedridden and only a strong woman can turn and lift her.'

'And when you become infirm, who will care for you out there?'

'There is always the Eternal Love of Jesus, Iria.'

'Forgive me, but tell me truly, are you afraid to return to the convent, Sister?'

'A little, perhaps, but more fearful of my own naked self. I cannot go back.'

'I do not understand this, Sister Eulalia.'

'I did not expect you to, but then you are strong and you have work and ties in the Church which absorb you continually. Why, it would not surprise me if you were chosen to go over into France. You know you have always wished to go to one of their centres of learning.'

'Only if the way was clear and the direction was obvious.'

'Well, so it seems to have come, for you. The Order at Grenoble have offered to receive five sisters from Spain. You heard that, did you not, to-day?'

'Yes. But I am prepared to stay where I am. Let others go.'

'But you will be sent, all the same. And there you will meet the famous man the writer – what was his name? – the one who came to Barcelona two years ago to the International Congress you were allowed to attend. Obviously, your work was considered very useful, or he would not have called on the Reverend Mother before he left to offer his compliments on our learning. Though of course he did not ask to see you. But she found him most distinguished, both profound and charming, she said.'

'There was no need for him to ask to see me. Really, what a child you are!' Iria spoke with some amusement. But Eulalia went on with her speculation.

'Why, perhaps you could study under his supervision. Should you not like that?'

'It is not what one likes. One grows out of that very soon. But what one can do most usefully.'

'Well, that is why you can do most usefully, I expect. And if it is what you like, also, as I suspect, well then, praise God for His special goodness to you.'

'And you regard your thoughts of leaving us as a mark of His goodness, too? How can you!'

'He is good to us all, though we cannot always get above the clouds to see His sun shining on us! But I am in a muddle. I have always been in a muddle. I am not made for thinking. It confuses me. Now when I am busy doing things, doing something needful for somebody or other, it all becomes clear, because I am doing and feeling, not thinking.'

'You have learned to pray and meditate.'

'Oh, I pray, but I don't meditate. No, no, I don't. I mean, not as you do. I try to keep my thoughts on the text and the devotions, but it's no use – they fly out of the window. I must be doing. I must be doing.'

'But you serve in the hospital.'

'There are plenty of sisters there. I want to work in the world, to be where the accidents are always cropping up, not where everything is ordered against men's mistakes and consequences.'

'Ah!'

'Don't withdraw yourself from me, Sister Iria. I need your support more than ever. Can't you see? It is because I am going. I am going!'

'Let us go to the Chapel. Perhaps Father Sebastian is still in the sacristy.'

'No, not yet. Let us talk to each other – truly, faithfully. Please, Sister Iria, help me. Help me.'

'How can I help you? You say you are resolved to go back into the world.'

'Out into the world, not back to it again. I never was in the world, that is the truth. But I have seen it now! They are in a muddle out there. I know what that is. Perhaps I can help them, in my own way, somehow.'

'Sister Eulalia, you are deceiving yourself. Isn't it the comforts, the luxuries you are attracted to – the sweet things, the shop-windows, the gossip ...'

'You are right to be stern with me. Yes, I do like the talk – yes, I know I do and perhaps the shops and the bustle – and the sweet-meats. Greed has always been my greatest sin, but, truly, that is all incidental to – to what I really want..'

'What is that, Sister?'

'The human love, Iria. The human love. God's Love is perfect and man's love is full of faults and failing. But I cannot live without it. I cannot.'

'You vowed to do so.'

'Then I lied. Whether in innocence or guilt, I do not know. But I vowed falsely.'

'Let us pray for heavenly mercy. I cannot help you.'

'Wait, wait. If only I could make you understand. You know how confused I always am. Have patience with me a little longer, I beg you!'

'Well, then, try to tell me, if you think it will help us both.'

'Sister Iria, in all our religious life, what have you come to find the most profound, the most solemn moments of all. I mean, what are the most precious times to you?'

'Why do you ask?'

'Shall I tell you what mine are?'

'Yes, do. Do.'

'The nights when it comes to my turn to keep watch in Chapel for the hourly prayers.'

'Probably that is true for us all.'

'It is true for you, then, Sister Iria?'

'Naturally', responded Iria gravely.

'Ah, then, perhaps at last you may understand that I am speaking truly.'

'I don't doubt that, at all.'

'You agree then that the thoughts one has at such times when one feels alone with God while all the rest are sleeping are not to be thrust lightly away?'

'Indeed, no.'

'Then you will not be shocked at what I am about to say?'

'Go on. I am listening.'

'And you will allow to my thoughts the truthfulness for me that your thoughts at such hours mean to you?'

'Yes. Go on.'

'As I go to pull the Chapel bell to mark the hour I say to myself 'How much more gladly would I rise up in the night to hush the crying of a child. I should not feel the cold of the floor, then, nor the roughness against my bare feet, nor the aching of hands and sides, nor need to console myself by the thought that I am storing up virtue of soul in Heaven, for I should be eager and glad to rise then, to perform that act of love. Yes! It is true. I must go on with what I am telling you. Listen, listen! But don't misjudge me. And when I chant the office of the night or dawn, I think of the cradle-tunes I might have sung to rock an infant's fears to sleep – and then out tolls the bell like a dirge for the dead – for those little ones that never lived. That is what my vocation hides, Sister Iria. It is a shroud to cover the little ones I never nursed – the little souls that never lived.'

'But why did you not confess to this before? Have you never spoken of it to anyone?

'What was the use? What was there to do? I could not leave whilst I was

'Why not?'

'That would have been base indeed. But now, how old am I? To be sure, forty-five, at least; my motives cannot be suspect or worse than they really are. I am free of that self-reproach. What did you say?'

'Nothing. Nothing.' Iria sighed.

'You are thinking how muddled I am. I have always been muddled. 'Eulalia sighed too, in turn. 'You are thinking I have spoiled two lives, my religious life and that other. Well, perhaps it is true. But God knows I have tried.' 'Yes, indeed, Sister.' Iria seemed reluctant to say any more on this point.

'Perhaps if I had had your wonderful brain, things might have been otherwise.'

'I am not so clear-headed as you seem to think.'

'I cannot believe that.'

'I assure you that the matters about which I most long to be clear are as dim to me as yours seem to be to you. For instance, when I am in the chapel alone – in my turn ...' Here Iria hesitated, then continued:

'Since you have confided in me, I will tell you my own perplexities. Sometimes at moments before I in my turn have pulled that bell, I have thought I could hear and feel – what it is I wish to hear and see.'

'And what is that?'

'I can find the words less easily than you can, Sister Eulalia.'

'I expect you want something more difficult!'

'Is it? I wonder! Yet like the human love you sigh for, I am sure it is everywhere, everywhere! It is the vibration of all life – of all life. Of life above and below. All life, all love, all existence is vibration. Can you feel that, Sister Eulalia?'

'I can feel it, perhaps, in a way, though not as you can, of course.'

'But would you not like to comprehend it?' Iria spoke eagerly now.

'If it would clear away the muddle in my head, yes.'

'Have you never longed so much to be lifted up on those vibrations that you have felt you were almost borne above your conscience life?'

'When I have nursed someone very ill, perhaps I have felt – something – but not – not a lifting above the earth. That would be ...' Eulalia faltered and dropped her voice to a whisper. 'Do you mean – you truly have felt that?'

'I have felt the power of those wings.'

'Do you mean – you have touched the angels!' Eulalia spoke timidly, as a child.

'I have not touched them. But they have been about me – very near – fluttering, vibrating, so that one could almost hear them, fluttering like great birds -beating the air, – lifting – lifting – always lifting upwards. Were they the everlasting arms? Ah! I am convinced of it, Sister Eulalia, all life is a vibration – light, sound – sensibility, echoes, waves – all our existence is a vibration circling round the throne of God. If one could but know! Oh, if only one could know!!!

'Is it not enough to feel them?'

'Ah! Perhaps that is my sin – this wanting to know – to discover tangible evidence – the intellectual proofs revealed in the words of others who have shared this sensation, however fragmentary. That, perhaps is my sin.'

'Why should it be? I put my finger on my pulse and say you must be right. But of course I never felt the angels' wings.'

'If you felt them once, you would sense them everywhere, become oblivious to all the world. Or conscious of them beating, however faintly, in all shapes of things.'

'Are you ever afraid to lose the certainty of it all?'

'How did you guess? Yes, I dread that they would leave me if I proved unworthy in any spot of thought or single action. I would die that they might live.'

'So that is why you never rest, but read, read, read continually?'

'It is the Truth of God to me, of God and Life. But let us pray and go to sleep. We shall need our strength tomorrow.'

'I will try not to give way to greedy wishes, Sister Iria. Perhaps I am to have strong temptations, so that I may acquire true resistance.' Eulalia spoke timidly again.

'You speak for us both, my Sister.'

'Forgive me, Sister Iria, but sometimes I used to think you were set to spy on me.'

'We are all guardians of one another. You of me, as I of you. You have set a check on my fault of intellectual pride many times.'

'I, Sister Iria? I?' Their voices melted into mingled sounds of mutual consolation.

'Yes, yes, indeed. But to our prayers. It is late. But first I will shut this window to.'

When I woke in the morning, the sun was high over the roof. It was late. In my first confusion of waking, I thought I heard the sisters still talking as I had heard them the night before. But it was the wood-pigeons cooing on the balcony outside.

There was a feeling of emptiness about that adjoining room. I went to my door and opened it. Yes, the room was empty. My nuns had fled.

I never thought I should see either of then again. But I was wrong. Later in the summer I met Sister Iria in a situation both grotesque and trying, but which she met with far greater dignity than I found myself able to command.

I was crossing the Pyrenees at Puiglerdá on my roundabout way to French Navarre. I was bent on an odd line of enquiry of which I had found no mention in musicological or folk-lore text-books. Among my Catalan friends I had chanced to learn that it had been an old custom for women to sing, with a kind of valorous joy, during the last moments of childbirth, and that though this tradition was supposed to have died out, it did in fact still exist, at least in isolated cases. I could never find out what song in particular, nor even exactly what kind of song women sang in these moments. 'Oh, an old song, naturally,' was the vague reply I usually received; 'an old Catalan song, of course …' And that was as much as I had learned.. But I did happen to remember that when Henry of Navarre had been born in the great Château of Pau his mother likewise had sung an old song to celebrate her triumphant achievement and release. So I was on my way over the mountains to see whether any traces of this curious tradition were still to be found over the border, or whether it was Navarrese in origin.

This route into France across the central Pyrenees is not as a rule nearly so frequented as that by Irun on the Basque coast or Port Bou on the Mediterranean. But on this occasion the frontier station was crowded. It soon became clear that rumours of the difficulties of getting out of Spain and of the intolerable delays, enquiries, and even searches had driven many people to take the longer route. There was a scare in the new Republic about the great sums of money and national treasures that were being unlawfully smuggled out of the country and new, rigid orders were being strictly enforced to prevent further leakages. Nuns, in particular, were objects of suspicion. 'Carrier-pigeons,' one Barcelona news-paper called them.

In these circumstances the evident nervousness of everyone at the frontier was natural enough. As we filed, step by step, into the long customs-shed and I saw how minutely luggage and all hand baggage were being turned out and examined, I began to wonder how long these new Republican officials would take to go through my wooden trunk of music and manuscript papers. There was room among them for all the bank notes left in Spain, if one were to believe the rumours of how much had already been smuggled away. So thought the first man who opened my box. He called his colleague and they began, tentatively, to lift up a few corners of the top sheets of music paper. This was going to be an interminable job. They looked up at me and

I looked down at them. 'Old music' I explained. 'Spanish music,' I added. They nodded their heads, thoughtfully, dubiously. 'Is there so much music in Spain?' ventured the older man. 'You should know,' I replied, with a smile, relieved at this sign of official relaxation. But then the younger man espied what seemed to him a curious object at the back of the trunk and with widening eyes began to draw it up to the surface – very, very carefully. His colleague exclaimed 'But what is this? What is this?' The man who was holding it, was turning it about, gingerly, when it slipped from his hands, fell on its side, and the catch opened. It was my metronome. It began to tick – tick – tick. The waiting crowd behind me suddenly ceased to mutter and exclaim with weary impatience. The ticking began to speed up; there was a dead silence all round. Then a gasp. Tick! Tick tick tick! I heard a scuffle. 'Bombas! Bombas! Hay bombas!' There was a flight for the doors, almost a panic. Stupidly, I lifted up the machine and laughed. My gesture was mistaken, and the metronome hurled from my hands by a prompt Guardia Civil. At this, my common sense returned. This was no time to enjoy one's appreciation of the absurd. Nerves were frayed, we were all on edge. So I grew serious at once, and began to explain the mechanism of the metronome and the purpose for which I carried it about with me. I think it was the ringing of the little bell to mark triple rhythms that finally convinced them, particularly when I hummed a *Guajira* with its changing beats and proved the essential usefulness of this additional device. There was quite a little gathering about me as I talked, beat time, and hummed snatches of tunes, and all seemed to be going well, and we were like children together, curiosity roused and satisfied. Unluckily, as the passengers filed back into their old places in the queues, covert smiles began to show on the faces of some better-informed travellers. Our new Republican zealots were nettled and stiffened into hostility again. The customs-official in chief was summoned. He gave a sharp order, and I was taken into the women's' section to be searched. I protested indignantly when I discovered the meaning of the command. Was I to be reduced to such total ignominy as a reward for my labours on Spanish music? It seemed most unjust. However, they took no notice of my indignation and began to toss my personal effects out of my valise in very unkindly fashion, with no regard for their value. But after a moment's hesitation it was after all decided not to search my person. But they took my new coat, my one great extravagance. 'Yes, made in Barcelona,' I replied to their enquiry. 'No, I have no bill to show you. Yes, it was made by a private modista. No, I cannot recollect her name. Maria Dolores de something.' The woman ran her hands over its seams again and looked at me. I was feeling annoyed, but what could one do? Suddenly she felt its beaver collar, stopped intently, and began vigorously to pull it about. 'Stop, stop!' I cried in alarm. That beaver collar had cost more money than I could really afford and she was pulling it out of shape in a most uncivil fashion. At this, another woman came up to take her share – and they called for the man posted at the door to stand forward as witness. Before him, they set upon my coat again and triumphantly told him to listen as they crumpled up the collar once more. It crackled! There! They looked at one another with genuine pride and satisfaction. It crackled. Here were bank-notes! Of course! Again I protested, but when I saw what they were about to do, I turned my back on them in vexed disgust, which I made no attempt to hide. A large pair of scissors was brought out – more like garden-shears than anything – and I shuddered as they began as they began to hack and rip up the fur.

Of course, the crackling proved to be from the buckram stiffening, as any self-respecting Spanish woman who did her own sewing would have known. But these were new-fangled, educated women officials. Well! my coat was ruined and to no purpose, for they were as chagrined as I was. But at least, my innocence was established, and I could now display my rage and contempt more openly.

'Estúpidas, estúpidas!' I stormed. 'Que estupidas mujeres tienen por aqui,' I cried to the man. I would not speak to them!

'Sssh! Sshsh!' hissed a warning voice behind me, from the women who were waiting their turn to be searched and examined. They did not want to be the victims of any sullen storm I might awaken. Evidently, everybody expected to be passed through the same experience now

But their women attendants looked a little abashed when the chief customs official came bustling in and I pointed out what harm they had brought to my new coat and what it had cost me only two days before when it had been finished and delivered to me. He called out a peremptory order and the woman who had ripped up my coat, brought out needle and thread from the drawer in her table – they seemed to be equipped for such incidents – and picked up my coat with an ill grace. In all my adventures in Spain I had never experienced such discourtesy. 'Black thread! Black thread for a red coat!' I demanded. 'What are you thinking of?' I demanded.

'We have no red thread,' she said shortly.

'You can have white, if you prefer,' said her colleague.

'Get on with it, get on with it,' snapped the man.

'They have missed the train now. There is plenty of time,' she retorted sourly.

There were groans and cries of exasperation on all sides at this thrust and the natural Spanish rebelliousness at authority suddenly burst out.

'Look how she is stitching that collar,' called out someone.

'What does it matter? It is ruined, anyway,' I replied, loudly.

'You should complain, you should complain. Why, whoever saw such sewing in Spain!'

The murmuring swelled almost to an outcry.

'What shame. What shame. It is a public outrage.' I heard people say. 'Just look at those poor nuns coming out of that place!' called out someone.

'Why, they have been stripped to the skin. This is outrageous. Poor things! Poor things! Look at them. As though they ever carry more money about them except for a night's lodging. Every decent person knows their order forbids it. This is shameful. This is shameful. What is this country coming to?'

A little group of nuns were being pushed out of a tiny, cell-like room whose door slammed behind them before they had barely passed out of it. They were still rearranging their clothing. Two or three of them were old and frail. All of them were trembling, though silent. All except one, and she stepped forward and stood in front of the others as if to screen and protect them from our sight. I recognised her at once; it was Sister Iria.

I moved towards her. But she looked at me as if I were a stranger and bent her head. I was not to speak to her. That was plain.

I watched her timid little flock move silently out of the customs· shed out on to the platform. A railway-porter moved forward to help them. But there was little to do and nothing, it seemed, to carry. Each carried a small wicker-woven basket large enough to hold the mid-day meal of a healthy road-mender, scarcely more.

Sister Iria said something to her little group and they were led away. But not towards the restaurants and rest-rooms, towards which all the other passengers had drifted. We had missed the express and there were hours to wait before the slower evening train would leave.

But the nuns walked slowly along the railway-track towards a deserted siding where there was an uncoupled second-class coach. There they mounted into the rear compartment, one by one. Sister Iria mounted last of all. Again she spoke to the railway-man, who nodded his head, and shut them in.

I never saw Sister Iria again. Was she on her way to Grenoble? I could have enquired. But, of course, I did not. There they stayed through the long, hot afternoon, though I daresay the time passed more quickly and evenly for them at their prayers than it did for the passengers in the restaurants, who found nothing to do except eat and argue and fume.

As for myself, I found a patch of green shade beyond the station, and there I reclined, simmering slowly until the quiet sense of remoteness which mountain air always brings cooled my wrath and exasperation. I called up the shade of George Borrow. What was it he had once written? I could not recall the exact words, but in feeling it amounted to this:

'Whatever your joy, whatever your pleasure may have been, however deep your love, devotion and passion and service for these Spanish people, somehow this country will contrive to send you packing, with indifference, ingratitude or injury.'

Did he not even add that Spain will give to that farewell the brutal force of a kick from a mule's hind-leg?

Well, it was a measure of one's love to feel that blow so keenly. And one would come again!

SCENES FROM SPANISH LIFE

Casals at Home

THE LETTER AWAITED ME IN Tarragona.

> 'Casals is at home again for the summer and has repeated his wish to meet you. Come as soon as you can. If you are still in Barcelona, the trains from there are not at all bad and you could easily manage a visit in one day. Bring your music, of course! There is nothing to do here, otherwise! But do remember this is the second time of asking!'

And so on.

I had revisited familiar treasures in Tarragona in less time than I had thought to spend. The tapestries – the manuscripts – the organist acquaintance, whose collection of local scraps, for which he could find no publisher, contained nothing new or strange, all these I had seen in less than two days. I went again to mass in the Cathedral with the letter in my pocket – how raucous and untenable that choir seemed! – and came out into the bright morning air thinking to go in search of a camionete that would take me on the Vendrell road in the direction of San Salvador, where Casals lived. I turned down the broad steps of the Cathedral and made my way to the right intending to cut across the vegetable market which blocked up most of the square. My senses noted gratefully the lively clean smell of fresh-cut cabbage though my thoughts were running on Casals' kind intentions towards an unknown young English girl.

At that time I was confident that I had all life before me and that a happy, fruitful existence would be the outcome of my study and sacrifice. Nevertheless, I recognised that the welcome of so famous a musician was a kindness to be prized. Indeed, I had been a little taken aback to learn that he had translated one of my earliest essays on Spanish music – on Granados – and had read it to some of Granados' oldest and closest friends. I had written that article more than a year ago, and with the swift development of youth I was already inclined to look back on it as something in the nature of an English high school-girl's effusion. But Casals and Granados had been intimate companions – how intimate I was not yet aware – and Casals had found sufficient sympathy of understanding in my first efforts to make him express the wish to make my acquaintance.

These pleasant thoughts were abruptly arrested, however. As I picked my way through the tumbled heaps of discarded cabbage leaves and cauliflower stalks, my path was crossed by the strangest apparition of gypsy beauty I had ever set eyes on. Nor have I ever since seen such a striking figure. She was much above six feet in height – possibly by three inches. Long-limbed, erect and silent she went striding along. Her dress was nondescript with age; it fitted closely to her neck and small bosom and was drawn tightly in to her high waist. The skirt swirled fairly voluminously about her lean, flat thighs. The tints of her skin ranged through a dull saffron to dark lemon and in her dark eyes and on her high cheekbones there was a tawny-orange gleam. Her hair was black and straight – drawn back from her face, but somehow it twirled down to curl in elfin locks over her narrow shoulders.

As she went she let her left arm drag behind her but seemed indifferent to the toad-like child which clung and dawdled on her extended fingers. This infant was an ugly, misshapen thing, and as the woman paused in her gait to stare at me, it promptly squatted down among the cabbage-leaves, hunched up its shoulders, and spat suddenly, venomously towards me, distorting its mouth in an effort to bespatter my dress. That stare she gave me was a magnificent expression of wild, untameable pride. She did not beg or attempt to wheedle me, and that put her apart from her own kind. When she had looked me up and down – what she made of my own expression as I gazed back upon her I could not fathom – she stepped forward on her way again and the child was tumbled and dragged along in the dirt by the force of her energy; she was unconcerned for its welfare as if it had been a log of wood she was hauling behind her. The men in the market place made room as she passed and nobody called after her, as I should have expected. The barrier was of her own making, that was evident. She would not beg, and she would not love. She was, indeed, unique among her scattered tribe.

Probably she lived in the cave-colony outside Tarragona. Probably

I could have discovered her story or followed and pieced together my observations on some thread of continuity, but as she passed down through the stalls and awnings she made a unique sight. No! I thought. You are not for framing and labelling. You have never been caught and tamed. Go your way, anonymously free! And so she went, slip-slopping in her down at heel slippers. The venerable atmosphere of ancient Tarragona and the air of ecclesiastical authority which hung about the place crumbled and dissolved into nothingness. The spirit of my Queen of the gypsy world was older and younger than their law.

The old coast road to Vendrell is a bumpy one and the old bus fell in to one pothole after another. At Vendrell I had over an hour to wait for the even more dilapidated bus which goes down to San Salvador of an evening, so I sauntered about the square and watched the local worthies sitting on their stone seats in the cooling air. It was dark when we reached the fishing-hamlet where Casals had bought land and made his gardens and I wondered for a moment whether they would be able to make me up a bed somewhere within the Ermita at such an hour and without notice. But I was not mistaken in my old friends. Juanet strode out from the back, wiping his hands in order to grasp mine in true peasant welcome as he recognised me, and calling out upon wife, mother and daughter to come, come quickly, that the English señorita was here again. Their welcome was genuine and I was soon installed. I had been here two years before during the autumn and these good people had not forgotten me. Visitors like me, it is true, were rare; that is to say, boarding guests, for the house was a primitive peasant home where no modern systems of plumbing might be expected. But Juanet owned a licence to sell spirits, and the fishermen dropped in here for their drinks as did the casual wayfarer who chanced to come that way.

Juanet also looked after the Ermita, the white-washed chapel that abutted on to his own premises. The Ermita – about the size of a stable – had been in existence since no man knew when. Sailors wrecked on the coast or fisherfolk saved from accident at sea came thither to pray and offer thanks.

Now and then pious humble people from Vendrell would come down for the day, first to pray, then to drink and water their donkeys and horses – if they came by cart – and finally to take lunch under the shadow of the boats drawn up on the open shore below the below the single line of white-washed cottages and huts. More privileged callers, and the local fishermen, went through the side-gate to the left and took their drams at the family outdoor table under the spreading vine that gave the patriarchal blessing of nature to the scene.

Juanet's wife, being an energetic woman and having only one child, had gone in for occasional catering in a modest way. She would cook a good omelette and serve it up briskly before you had begun to drum idly with knife and fork to pass the time of waiting away. Her chickens were plumper than the usual run of Spanish poultry. That was because Juanet ran the kitchen garden in a judicious, perspicacious Catalan way, and there was always abundance on the plot for family, visitors, hens and pigs alike. They had orange and lemon trees, grapes and figs. He had, too, a shrewd taste in wines and spirits, so that the Ermita was not to be despised as far as eating and drinking were concerned, even if you were rather fastidious about a night's lodging. But there were no hotels of any description for many miles around. This, in fact, was the attraction to the handful of families who came for a month or two in the summer. The fishermen's cottages could not house more than half a dozen groups of relations, so the company was entirely confined to the near intimates of Casals, round whose estate the activity of San Salvador now revolved.

There was nothing picturesque or striking about the place whatever, nor could it boast at all of having any conveniences and rural amenities. There were no coves, or caves, or rocks and pools, nor cliffs, scarcely a sand-dune, even: only a long, straight, open beach, opposed to wind and storm in winter and bare to the glaring sun throughout the long hot summer. There were no mountains within near range – Montserrat was quite a distance away – only flat, stony land, half-heartedly cultivated in patches here and there and a few miles inland the modest little unindustrialised country town where Casals was born. With all the natural beauties of Spain to choose from, it seemed strange that he had settled upon such an ordinary spot, devoid of all those overtones of tradition for which so many part of Spain are justly famous; undertones, of course, are more rare in the Peninsula. I wondered, curiously, but not inquisitively, what the inner attractions were that had drawn him back again and again from his world-wide travels and tours. His roots went very deep somewhere hereabouts, I felt sure.

I ate at the family table under the vine that night. Juanet brought out a special sandia in my honour and as we lingered over dessert I praised its crisp but juicy rose-pink flesh, till the oil-lamp was lit and smoked away as I had remembered. The lizards darted up and down the white wall behind Juanet's head as before and rustled in out of the thickening vine-leaves overhead. Juanet's wife confided to me that the figs were ripening well and that I must stay longer this time in order to enjoy them, which I promised very readily to do.

Juanet's old mother had lost two more teeth, as she demonstrated beyond dispute to me – teeth were the milestones by which she measured the passing of time, by the way – and she was therefore more unintelligible though none the less garrulous, than ever. And Juanet's little daughter was now a pretty, silky-haired monkey of sixteen; glossy, dark and shapely like an unblemished olive.

Soon after supper, in strolled the coastguardsman, as I had hoped.

'Look who's here', called Juanet to him, in great good humour.

'Oh, he doesn't want to see me', I laughed. 'I can see the question mark all over his face: 'Has she brought that guitar with her?'' Juanet chuckled and roared and slapped the coastguard on the back.

'She has, though. She has!'

And the coastguard, beginning to grin with satisfaction sidled down on the bench beside Juanet, carefully leaned his rifle behind him against the ledge, pushed back his peaked cap and unbuttoned his tunic to the waist.

'The señorita has come back for bad times, though', he muttered. He suffered from his liver and always took a poor view of things, except when he held a guitar in his hands.

'Well, yes, we thought you'd be at war with Italy by this time', explained Juanet. This was the year of Mussolini's Abyssinian campaign and the threat of sanctions.

'I hope not,' I said vaguely.

'I wasn't thinking of that', put in the coastguard. 'It's what's going on here right under our noses; that worries me!'

'Indeed?' I looked round at them all quickly now.

'I hear your gun licence was delivered to you today', the coastguard turned to Juanet.

'Yes, this morning', replied Juanet with a slight shadow on his joviality.

'What are they going to let you shoot, now Juanet?' I said lightly, trying to restore the festive mood of our reunion.

Juanet got up. He was heavier than before, I noticed, but as sturdy as ever. 'I'll show you. I'll show you', he said and went in to the little bar and fished about among a pile of papers under the till. Then he came out again and spread a couple of official-looking documents on the table and we all bent over and peered at them in the dimness of the oil lamp while he began to trace out the lines with his thumb and read slowly aloud for the benefit of his mother who could not see at all, and for his wife, who read with difficulty. I suspected that the coastguard was not so well grounded in his letters as his post supposed him to be, either.

Juanet's new licence gave him authority to shoot at any suspicious seeming stranger who did not respond satisfactorily to interrogation put to him in lawful manner.

'Ay, Jesús! Ay, Jesús!' whispered the women. 'And only one man in the house at night'. Juanet looked at me in amusement at this and swelled his great chest. 'It would be a bold rascal who tried to force this house while I'm master in it', he said with a gleam of battle in his dark blue eyes.

'Yes, indeed', I said, admiringly.

'Well, I for one am glad you took my advice and got out those old beams to put behind the doors at night', said his wife pointedly.

'They were saying this afternoon that Casals was enquiring about the price of two wolfhounds in Vendrell last week', he said hastily to the coastguard. 'Do you know anything about it?'

'It's likely enough', said the coastguard, draining his glass.

'Hmm', said Juanet.

'That dog of yours is a bit fat to be of use in a scuffle, Juanet'.

'Well, yes, I'd been thinking so myself just lately', said our host, cautiously. 'He's been a fine fighter in his day, of course'.

Juanet sighed involuntarily and refilled the coastguard's glass, keeping the score in his head, as was his way among friends.

In his day Juanet had been the most famous, the most hardy and bold smuggler on all the eastern coast from the Pyrenees down to Cartagena. He was now a respectable property owner, prompt with his taxes and guardian of the Ermita. All that past had been forgotten except the glory as it lingered, and Juanet kept that alive whenever he could. I had grown accustomed to many odd juxtapositions in Spanish life but the spectacle of Juanet telling racy stories of his past enterprises to the local coastguardsman entrusted with the suppression of smuggling in this area of Catalonia was one that never palled. This particular crony was a saturnine, low-browed Aragonese, weedy in form, but bristling with thick moustachios of a most war-like character, which deceived nobody. He was always complaining of his lot in having been posted out of his native region, and whenever anyone spoke in Catalan, which was more often than not, he suspected treason, sedition and bloodshed. But he was an excellent foil to Juanet's joviality and on the guitar he was master of a fine crispness of fingering, which was an exhilaration of the spirit to all who heard him play. Unluckily, he was always in debt, nothing of an alarming extent, but his month's pay was mortgaged continually ahead in dribs and drabs of petty expenditure. His most constant complaint was against his wife, whom he accused under his breath nearly every evening of presenting him with a new child every year, solely to stop him from gathering money enough to purchase a guitar. The poor man had never owned an instrument of his own and was therefore dependant on chance encounters for his musical needs, for it was more than pleasure to him. I believed that all his irritability and excess bile was due to this deprivation. Well! For the next few weeks he would be happy and we should have marvellous evenings while the lizards cast their darting shadows up and down the wall and the oil lamp smoked and flickered. Once more the cocks would be crowing in the distance before we separated for bed.

On the morrow I did not need to make any formal calls to announce my arrival. In fact I received my first visitors whilst taking my breakfast in the shade of the venerable fig-tree by the cistern where Juanet drew little stoups of water for his marrow-beds and pursued a colloquy with me as he marched up and down. But he withdrew to the raspberry canes at the bottom of the garden when my summer visitors came in search of me and I was drawn into music chatter from the many corners of the international concert world.

Casals would be happy to see me at his house that evening, I was told. Meanwhile there was the day to fill in, and I would bathe with them. My new Mexican sky-blue suit of shorts and over-jacket was much admired. The carrier who kept an open stall by the beach during the summer offered to find me a wide-brimmed peasant hat bound with a matching braid and within two hours reappeared triumphantly from Vendrell with a Mexican high-crowned shape trimmed and edged with the same shade of blue. The children clapped their hands with glee and at once I was an established member of the tiny colony of holidaymaking musicians and their little ones. There was a violinist from Barcelona, a conductor from Madrid, a soprano lieder singer and Eisenberg from New York. Casals' brother's children were there and one or two close friends, connected with the organisation of his orchestra. Everyone was supposed to be preparing autumn programmes but in effect we were usually together on the sands by noon, if not before.

Eisenberg was rather worried about Casals.

'He is working himself to death over a new concerto, and in my opinion it's not worth the trouble he's taking'.

'Do you mean a new work?' I was surprised to hear him, because there was a general impression that nowadays Casals kept his gifts for the interpretation of the established masters.

'Well, it's supposed to be a new work. But it's by an Englishman, if you see what I mean'. I laughed. I saw what he meant, exactly.

'Didn't I tell you?', said the soprano. I shook my head. I explained that I was not often in England these days and didn't know the current gossip of what was going on behind the scenes there.

'Well, he will probably tell you about it tonight', said the violinist. 'Look at his finger tips when you get the chance. Eisenberg is perfectly right. If a man with Casals' technique has to cut his pads nearly to ribbons in order to get his effects out of the score, then the music can t be worth much, in my opinion'.

'What a place to spend the summer', spluttered the conductor. 'Do you know, we went all over Vendrell yesterday trying to get some ice to put in our naranjada, and did we hear even the suspicion of a chink? No! Not even a splinter! Well, each to his own taste, I suppose'.

'It's home to Casals', naturally', I ventured.

'Naturally', was the generally vague reply, and we left it at that.

I returned to the Ermita for lunch. The naranjada there was as cold as spring water. Juanet had learned much in his travels, including the proper temperatures at which to keep his wares in the windowless little bar.

The family seemed pleased to hear that I was going to spend the evening at Casals' home.

'It was a pity you missed him last time', said Juanet's wife. 'He was up at Montserrat, you know. He often goes up there for retreat for a few days when he comes back from abroad'.

'Yes, so I have heard. And he always comes back to his old home'.

'And why should he not?' said Juanet energetically. 'He has the best vines for miles around. I should be a proud man if I had those. Besides, he was bred and born in Vendrell. Look at me! I've come back, haven't I, and I've travelled a bit in my time, too!' That was conclusive.

'I remember the first time I saw him ...', the old woman leaned across the table towards me.

'Oh, where was that?' I asked quietly.

'Why, here, in his mother's arms', she said unexpectedly.

'Here! In the Ermita, do you mean?'

'Yes, indeed. She brought him all the way down from Vendrell in her arms, her first day's outing. In the old days, it was always that way. They don't do it any more, though.'

'A few, now and then', said Juanet. 'But only now and then. Why, there was that couple with the baby at Easter, if you remember, came for mass. They were from Vendrell'.

'Oh, you mean his mother brought him down to the chapel? I see.'

'She brought him other times, too', said the old woman. 'I've seen them.'

'I see!' I said.

'Surely!' she said emphatically. 'And that's why he's prospered. Casals never forgot what his mother had done for him when she brought him up – And that's why he's prospered. And that's why so many go to rack and ruin these days, because they forget and are not mindful of their parents in their old age!' The old lady looked at Juanet, then folded her hands in her lap, under her apron, and sat back in her chair. She had said her say.

I went across the lane to Casals' house in rather a different frame of mind to what I had expected. The little group who were taking me to call were gathered at the corner. They were all famous in the international sphere, but I noticed as we mounted the steps to the door that they lowered their voices almost imperceptibly.

As we paused on the threshold, the musician from Barcelona turned to me and said;

'Let me see, where did you last hear Casals perform?'

'But I have never heard him play!' I exclaimed.

The looks of consternation on their faces were comically identical.

'But this is impossible!' He looked quite aghast. 'How can we introduce you?' They all looked quite nervous.

'I am sorry', I said, 'but that is how it is. Of course, since I came into Spain I have heard him conduct a dozen times at least, and attended rehearsals too, but you see, in England, I ...I ...' Before I could explain the situation, we saw Casals advancing towards us along the corridor and we were all silent. He took my hand and drew me in before the others.

'What were you saying?' His voice was pleasantly kindly.

Someone poked me warningly in the back. But I was not going to be falsely polite to the man who had already shown such interest in a stranger. 'I was explaining to our mutual friends why I have never heard you play'. I began with resolution, but dropping off into a faltering voice as I grew aware of the quiet dignity with which he was looking at me. 'You see, as a student in London, I was always entirely dependent on the free tickets I could get for concerts. Usually, of course, there are spare seats every night of the week. But never an empty one at any of your performances, you see! Not a single place, ever!'

Casals looked surprised for a moment; then he laughed, and looked around at the abashed expressions of our mutual acquaintances. Then he looked again at me. 'I see!' he said, beginning to smile.

'I have had to save every penny since I was a child in order to come to Spain to study. Of course, I have heard you conduct many times in these last three years here – whenever that was possible! – but, well, people complain that you do not play your cello so often at home as you do abroad ...' Here I got another sharp poke in the back. I was telling tales. Casals looked at me again, rather more intently. Then he smiled again, and we moved forward down the bare corridor.

'Well, as a matter of fact', he began slowly, 'I never play my best in England. It is a pity, because I have many good friends there, but the climate does affect one's instrument, you know. But come in, come in, all of you.' In we went to the double music-room that looked over the seashore. Family introductions were made, but before I could attend to anyone else, Casals drew me into the inner room where his little upright piano stood. 'I have some things to show you. You know who that is, of course?' He led me to a corner behind the door where a portrait in oils hung.

'Oh yes, of course! That is Granados'.

'Yes. That is Granados'. We stood in silence looking up at the painting. 'It is quite a good likeness', he added after a few moments. 'You would like to see the cast of his hands, I daresay.'

'Oh, have you those?' I exclaimed, naively.

'Yes, indeed, we were very close friends! Here! Look!'

I was disconcerted by the long fragility of the hands, and said so.

'But you stressed the delicacy of his nature in your essay, I think?'

'Yes, but these are almost the hands of a woman!'

'They are strong, all the same. Look at the muscular development, here and here!' His friends sat about and chatted or listened as he talked to me. Their expressions showed that I was being unusually favoured and I felt self-conscious. I began to perceive that I lacked the practised social manner which would have enabled me to steer a middle course between moments of excessively expressed gratitude and awkward silences when I felt I had just said too much. However, Casals continued to talk to me, as though my inexperience was quite natural.

'I liked what you said about the influence of his mother on his musical formation', he said, suddenly. 'That was quite true, I think.'

At this, it was my turn to look rather more intently at him that I had yet ventured to do. I remembered what the old woman had said that afternoon. 'I guessed a little; that is, I put two and two together. After all, in Spain, the musical taste of children is formed very early in the home where mothers and nannies and aunts and elder sisters are always singing snatches of this and that', I suggested.

'Yes. That is true. You have made good use of your time among us.'

'Well, I had the good luck to spend my first six months in the Montañesa and along that coast where his mother's people came from, and it did strike me that the cadences in his music look back to those early influences. I have a theory that cadences express the conservative elements in our natures, perhaps. But it was just luck. I do get that kind of luck, quite often. I call it the divine accident', I added in a burst of confidence, for he had listened quietly to what I had to say. 'One feels one is on the right path, when that happens, somehow', I ended.

Casals nodded. 'Yes, I know what you mean. For instance, I am not sure if you know that I played in the first performances of several of his works?' No, I did not. He went on: 'I had not seen him for some time. You know how it is with musicians – you go your separate ways all over the world and then – in 1915 during the war, it was – I happened to be in New York the night of the first performances of the Goyescas. His last work, his last appearance ...'

'Oh, you were there? You saw it? You heard it?'

'Yes. As I had heard his earliest works so I heard his last. Well, that was one of your divine accidents, perhaps, don't you think?'

'Do tell us, Casals!' The others gathered round to hear him describe that evening of romance and wonder in the New York Opera House. 'Yes, there was a touch of perfection about that night', he concluded. We were silent as we thought of Granados' fate, torpedoed and drowned in the English Channel on the last stage of his voyage back to Europe. He spoke of Granados' presentiment and of presentiments in general.

'But you know of that', Casals said briefly. 'Let us have a little music, and then we will talk another time about Granados, if you wish. By the way, did your concert tour in Germany go well?'

'Unfortunately, it didn't go at all', I confessed.

'I am sorry to hear that. What happened? When I was reading your article I was told that you were going to sing Spanish songs there?'

'Yes, I was invited, but it seemed I had to pay my own fare to the frontier and back; I hadn't anticipated that, and I couldn't raise the money in time. I had only enough to bring me back to Spain, and I had to keep that, of course. There is still so much I have to do here.'

'That seems a pity.' Again it was our mutual friends who seemed embarrassed by my excessive candour.

'Yes, it was', I continued, as he seemed to expect me to go on. '1 hoped the BBC would have given me an engagement or two and then I could have managed. But I'm afraid I made the mistake of overvaluing the musical intelligence of the BBC representative who heard my specimen programme. They didn't seem to think that sixteenth-century Spanish romances sung to a plucked guitar were of sufficient musical interest to introduce to their public; they were all manuscripts 1 had copied in Spain, too, as I explained. I'm afraid they didn't even realise what it was all about. I took it for granted they would know. It was only afterwards I found out that one of the jury was a young man fresh from Cambridge who had just attended a three months summer course on the Spanish language and the other one only a woman accompanist to popular ballad singers!' Casals looked a little worried, so I said promptly, 'However, I got an apology, in writing!'

'But no engagement?'

'No, no engagement. But I am told it is much more difficult to get an apology out of them, than an engagement, especially a written apology!'

There was a general laugh at this.

Then came the surprise. Casals went to the piano, sat down and opened the lid. Then he called to his sister-in law.

'As this is an evening in memory of Granados, I thought we would give you a little music. Are the children there?' Yes, the children carne in.

'My nephews and nieces', he explained. I already knew them. They grouped themselves on either side of the piano, watching him obediently.

He struck a few chords, quietly, unimpressively. The piano was not in very good tune. Spanish pianos seldom are. But that to acute musical minds in Spain is a matter of little importance. To carry the absolute pitch in one's mind is the essential thing. It is a fact worth noting, I think, that the piano is, relatively speaking, the Cinderella of instruments in the Peninsula. The reason is not far to seek. It contrives with ingenuity to obscure the fact that, fundamentally, it is unable to produce a living note; for the Spaniard, to whose dramatic nature of whole life and death of any experience – even of a single note of music – is of first importance, the inability of the piano to reproduce in sound this elementary and elemental quality relegates it to the plane of a substitute and accessory.

In an undertone, Casals' voice gave the cue and the children bent their heads a little in concentration, then opened their mouths and began with simple directness to sing the service of the mass. It was Casals' faith to which they gave voice, intimately, steadily. The work was purely devotional in character and belonged to no school or period. There was enough music to support the contemplative communion of the text and no more. I thought of Mozart, Bach, Beethoven, Brahms, Verdi, Faure, Berlioz even. These were all musicians first, pouring the Church service into their musical moulds of personality. Casals was an anonymous worshipper; his music was simply the breath of a humble and dutiful faith, the human vibration seeking its point of rest in the Sublime. The children's faces were inexpressive, but their young voices were clear and slight, even subdued, as they watched his guiding beat, the occasional gesture of his right hand as he lifted it from the keys.

Nobody spoke at the conclusion of the little family service, and after a pause the children came round and bade us all goodnight. Then they embraced their uncle, still seated at the piano, and went away to bed. Only then did he close the instrument and lead us into the outer room where conversation became more general.

The international tension between Italy and the League of Nations was the topic most earnestly discussed and Gibraltar was mentioned, with an apologetic glance at me. The Italians were trying to embroil the Spaniards by rubbing salt into the old wound of our occupation of the Rock.

'Mare Nostrum!' exclaimed Casals vigorously, moving towards the centre of the company. 'And what, may we suppose, will be the fate of Gibraltar if England is obliged to give it up'? Speaking as a Spaniard, I could easily name the powers that will begin fighting or manoeuvring for its possession. Nobody in the present situation imagines that it will fall into absolute Spanish control! And speaking again as a Spaniard, I would like to ask what advantage there would be in seeing Gibraltar fall into any other hands than the British? It is only since the British Navy has kept order in the Mediterranean that the Mediterranean has known peace and justice – and – and – that Spain has always been able to behave on the complete assurance that she always receives her fair due. Can you imagine the intolerable situations that would arise in our internal affairs were any other power to be in control down there, or what incidents would be provoking us in Gibraltar and along our coasts if we were to be in nominal possession of the Rock again? This is NOT the time to amend the status quo!'

I looked at Casals with admiration. These were brave words uttered at such a time of crisis before a group of international celebrities. There was a general feeling – it was widespread – that the Italians were in fair shape to beat the British. We were known to be weak, uncertain and impoverished, while the Fascist temper and show of energy were intimidating many people, particularly south of the English Channel. In America the Italian vociferation was convincing public opinion that great changes in the balance of power were being initiated in Rome.

I left Casals' home that night with an impression that there was a strength of character in this man which went beyond the genius of his music.

'Come again on Sunday", he said as I left. I lingered a little, trying to catch a glimpse of the pictures hanging on the walls; they seemed to be chiefly modern French or Italian, perhaps some of the smaller landscapes were Catalan. 'If you are interested in painting, I can show you some other, then', he added. I could only murmur a few words of gratitude, but I hoped he could read the expression, which must surely reflect in my face, the emotion I felt at heart.

'Well, what do you think of him?'

'Yes, do give us your first impression', my friends insisted.

'Why', I said slowly, as we stood on the corner of the lane, 'Why, I think he is naturally a modest man who has acquired a proper regard for his own genius! What stars you have here! And listen to the grillos! They sound like the vibration of burnished silver. Unamuno is right; there is an almost mystical fervour and intensity about their chirping!'

'Bona nit! Bona nit!'

'Ara fa nones! Ara fa nones!' we laughed, fumbling with the traditional Catalan goodnight sayings and parted till the morrow.

When the sounds of their voices had died away, I stood in the road below the Ennita and looked at the brilliant sky and listened to the grillos again. The stars seemed to tremble with the light that charged and pierced them, whilst by the roadside the hidden insects seemed to glow and shine by the fervour of the noise with which they shook. Then I perceived that they were all one – sight and sound; vibrations from our familiar earth and rays from other worlds. Truth was here and now, as it had always been and one supposed would always be. Might as well make one's home here as anywhere, I thought, as Juanet lit the candle that saw me up the narrow winding stair to bed.

The street in Vendrell where Casals lived as a child was a quiet one. The exterior of its houses gave no clue to the life within, as I was able to see when the wedding of one of Juanet's second cousins, whose parents rented a corner shop there, brought me an invitation to meet the bride and to inspect her presents. The young bridegroom was a leading player in the Vendrell football team and assisted his father in the shop. The bride's family were millers in a small way, storing the sacks of wheat in the lower part of their home, which was close by. When we clambered up the steep dark stairway to the front living room, the impression of the entrance, deep in layers of fine white dust and milling sacks left me unprepared for the comfort of the home upstairs. Here was Catalan comfort, solid, prosperous. The great carved sideboard was laden with fruit and sweetmeats displayed in silver and cut-glass dishes. The table linen was fine and hand-drawn and embroidered with restrained designs. There was abundance and

cheerfulness everywhere throughout the house. The bride was espe-
cially eager to show a young English girl her treasures and led me
away to where the bridal bed lay already stacked with household
gifts. She showed me the contents of her wedding chest, and my gen-
uine cries of admiration for the silks and satins she had had enriched
with what seemed like years of stitchery gave the mother great plea-
sure and we became friends immediately. I noticed that the young
couple had been given several sets of well-printed books and a gramo-
phone for which they had themselves chosen all the records. Their
selection was creditable to their taste, and I came away with Juanet's
daughter thinking of Casals' family background and of this steady,
durable standard of living that had been about him in his
childhood ...

There was quite a frolic at the Ermita that evening – sedate but
warm-hearted. There were no international celebrities present, but
our coastguard turned up prompt and early and seized the guitar
without a word. Several local acquaintances sauntered in by ones and
twos and when I said no, I had never tasted apricot brandy, Juanet
brought out a flagon and pushed glasses of it all round the table
where we lounged and sat expectantly.

My boast on my earlier visit that I knew fifty-two Jotas – one for
every week of the year – had been substantiated – and what was more
– I had brought fifty-two instrumental variations, which was much
more difficult to amass – and I was generally admitted to be hard
nowadays to catch out with some unknown song. There were great
clappings of hands and drummings of heels during the music-making
and roars of laughter at the intervening anecdotes that frightened the
lizards and nearly put out the light. Juanet's wife brought out anoth-
er lamp, which served only to deepen the shadows and lit up nothing
except perhaps the lively glances of our eyes. Juanet's little daughter,
I noticed for the first time, had an admirer. I saw both father and
mother glance sharply at her once or twice, and at the young man
who had appeared unannounced with a bicycle, it seemed, for the
first time. The young couple said nothing to each other the whole
evening, and it was that, perhaps, that gave significance to their meet-
ing. However, the young stranger very properly kept in the back-
ground and made no attempt to make himself heard in conversation
or song. She was still very young, but on this evening she seemed to
pass quietly from one stage of her life into consciousness of another.

She seemed also to be more assiduous in helping her mother than before. She had always been inclined to sit alone and say nothing until called upon, but now she went hither and thither behind her mother, anticipating her duties with a new alacrity. I think she knew that the young man's eyes were able to follow her more naturally as she moved here and there.

Juanet began to talk of the old days.

'Ah! It's the horse that makes the man!' he exclaimed. 'There's nothing like having a good horse between your knees to give a man confidence when he goes into a new town on a dangerous business. It gives a rider the advantage over the man on foot. The men look at the horse and judge you to have substance and the women look at the man, because they see he knows how to be firm with a kittle creature!'

'Did you engage in many dangerous errands?' I enquired.

'Well, as it happened, I never fell into any trap set for me, so whether it was all so very dangerous I can't truly say, but by the money they paid me, it proved not many men could be found for the jobs I used to tackle! There was spice in it, of course.'

Yes, one could see there had been plenty of spice in the adventures, by the triumphant gleam, which still lit up Juanet's eyes. He must have fascinated many women, I thought. Even now, at sixty-one, bulky and stiff as he was growing, there was a stir of excitement about the way he sometimes moved that made the gait of younger men seem stale and uninviting.

'There was certainly money in it in the old days', said the carrier. 'Yes, of course. Juan March paid well even in his earliest days. That was the secret of his success. He never grudged paying a good price to get the best men.'

'They say he's given up since he went into politics', said the coastguard. 'Do you think it's true, Juanet?'

'Juan March give up? Not he! Besides, how is he to pay for his politics without running a few things up and down and in and out?'

This argument was solidly irrefutable, and everyone nodded.

'Well, you got out of it, Juanet, and not too badly', said the carrier.

'Not too badly', agreed Juanet, with sudden caution. 'And now I'm on the local council; with this new licence to kill at sight. They don't give that licence to so many in the parish, you know.'

'Shows you're considered to be a man of substance, Juanet, that's what it means', retorted the carrier meaningly.

'No', said Juanet. 'It means we're heading for worse times than ever. That's how I see it. Where do they all come from, these fly by night prowlers? There's no decent beggars left in the place!'

'It's what I keep telling you', said the coastguard. 'They've turned them all loose out of prison, that's how it is. The jails are empty!'

'No', said Juanet, shaking his head. 'It's not all that. There's something got loose. There were always curs, but in the old days they slunk round the corners when they saw decent men coming along the road. Now, they turn and bare their teeth at you. It's something in the air; it's turning them dangerous.'

'It's bad', agreed the carrier, reflectively. 'It's bad, and it will have to get worse before it gets better. It always does, you know.'

'Well', said Juanet's wife, there's one comfort, there's not much in San Salvador to tempt evil-doers.'

'Don't you be too sure', said the coastguard. 'What about Casals' place?'

'Someone might take a fancy to the statues in his garden', suddenly exploded the old woman, with a shrill cackle. There was a gale of guffaws at this. 'What statues?' I asked innocently.

They all laughed again, paused, then went off into even louder fits of merriment than ever. The men were uproarious, and I began to wonder what it all meant.

'Perhaps Casals will show her when she goes to call on Sunday!' said the old woman with unexpected glee.

'Mother!' cried Juanet's wife. 'How can you forget yourself so?' She sounded angry. But the old lady threw her apron over her head and shrieked and rocked and heaved with merriment past all restraint. I began to wonder whether Casals had acquired any Epsteins or models of the Picasso school when a half-phrase of the carrier enlightened me. I realised then that San Salvador was indeed a Garden of Eden and innocence into which the Tree of Knowledge had not yet been transplanted. The statues in Casals' garden were classical, undraped subjects; that was all; but these neighbours of his had never seen their like before. It was clear that living here Casals was still surrounded by the simplicity of outlook of his childhood.

The child visitors to San Salvador seemed to fall into two groups. The elder ones went sailing all day long and we saw little of them until nightfall. The younger boys and girls, however, ranging up to about ten years old or thereabouts, had to devise their own amusements when they tired of paddling and splashing each other in the water. Among them there was one small girl, not more than seven, who attracted attention easily enough, because she was always looking for it, or so it seemed to me. Carmencita was certainly extremely pretty and the idol of her mother and nurse. She had a pale skin and deep gold hair that was always elaborately curled. Her eyes were grey and she existed in a perpetual thrill of excitement.

I still remember my first view of her leading a wedding group along the track behind the fishermen's cottages. The bridegroom was a chubby innocent boy of her own age, stolid and wondering. They had found him a miniature frock coat and top hat from somewhere, and he carried one white glove between his folded hands. Carmencita was the bride and she was draped in a cream silk muslin curtain whose heavy fringe she had carefully arranged to fall down her back. Her arms clashed bangles at every gesture as she recited at a high pitch the first lines of a poem that she rendered thus:

'La señora Luna ...quiere casar

Con un pajarito ...' She would get so far then pause and stumble and start again, each time setting the pitch of her treble voice higher and hitching up her curtain veil and assuring herself that the wreath of flowers on her head was still set at a becoming angle. She was the Lady Moon, of course, and the little boy groom was the little bird whom she wished to marry

Behind them came a priest. He was the oldest boy in the party and had been invested in a sack slit up the sides and with a hole for his head to pass through. When Carmencita stopped for breath he would intone from his prayer book. Behind him came a miscellaneous bevy of bridesmaids, straggling in ones and twos. Some of them carried bunches of weed-grass and wild flowers wilting and drooping as flowers usually do when clutched in the hot, tight grasp of little children. Occasionally they responded to the priestling's chant with a quavering kind of intoning, but they immediately broke off when Carmencita turned round and commanded silence for her resumption of poetics. The procession went up and down the lane then up and down the beach, then back as far as the carrier's stall. Finally, a special performance was added for my especial benefit. Carmencita was quivering all over as she saw that I watched her closely.

All at once she stopped short and gave a shrill long squeal. 'They've caught a sea-snake!' she cried. 'They've caught a sea-snake!'

She tore off her veil and the wreath toppled into the dust. 'Look! LOOK!' She pointed in the direction of two fishermen's wives – enormous women – who with much difficulty were staggering along under the weight of a huge tub over whose sides water slopped convulsively.

'It's a great eel, I do believe', said the priest, throwing off his sack and stuffing the prayer-book into his jacket. 'They're going to my house first! No, they're not! They're going to yours, Carmencita. Come on! Come on!'

'Come and see! Come and see!' she squealed, jumping up and down, clapping her hands and ordering everybody al-out. 'Come and sit on the steps of MY house, I tell you. Nannie! Nannie!' She rushed and capered along while her curls bobbed up and down on her shoulders. 'Where's my chair? Where's my chair? Bring my chair, Nannie!' Nannie obediently brought out Carmencita's little wooden chair. 'Put it there! No! There! There, I tell you!' commanded the little tyrant and Nannie obeyed like a slave to her mistress's whim.

'There!' cried Carmencita with intense satisfaction. 'Oh, isn't this fun! Oooh! Isn't this marvellous! Now we *shall* enjoy ourselves! Now we *shall* enjoy ourselves!' And she beat on the arms of her chair with a force one would scarcely have thought a small girl could raise.

'They're coming! They're coming!' chanted the boys joyfully, and slowly, laboriously the women drew near with their prey.

'Sit down, all of you. How can I see when you stand up?' called Carmencita. 'Sillies!' The children sat down on the steps while she again beat on the arms of her chair like a Roman emperor's daughter waiting for the game to begin in the arena below her.

Yes, it was a great black eel. Poor, dumb, writhing creature! I shrink to tell what awaited you now. They dragged you out of the tub. They laid you gasping on the bare, hot earth. You coiled and glistened in the glaring light. You leaped and twisted your shiny joints while the children shrieked for glee. In vain you sought to dive and thrust yourself down out of sight. The earth was not your kindly nurse and natural element!

'What will you have?' called one of the women to Carmencita's mother's cook. She considered and called out something and held up two fingers. The other woman drew out a curved knife from under her coarse apron. Carmencita turned pale and drew in her breath. 'AH! AH!' she shuddered, and moved her chair forward to the extreme edge of the steps where she could command an even closer view.

To my horror, whilst it was still fully alive, the fish-wife swooped down and cut off about a foot and a half from the tail end of the eel, which stopped its twisting, lifted its head high in the air from side to side as though looking for some witness to this unbelievable stroke of anguish, then, slumped down slivering dully, an inert mass, twitching feebly and still more feebly. Then the other woman splashed water over the mutilated body and slowly it revived. Once more the agony began, this time earth-contemning in its horror and pain. The maimed coiled thing beat itself upon the hard earth – beat and beat – and beat again – till we heard the thuds of our own heart-throbs sicken and slow to that pulse of death. What is the terror that lies in the agony of a voiceless living creature than can make no cry in its pain, no appeal to mercy? Does it mean that there is no listening Heaven above?

Again the knife descended. Another joint was severed and laid bare. And now blood trickled out from the entrails in a slow, sick ooze, only that red vein showing movement as the great eel at last lay still. Thank God, it is over! I cried.

But no! There were other prospective customers. Again the water was slapped over the stump that remained – dusty now and slimed – and again it glistened in a black shiny half circle, but feebly, unconscious now, indifferent to the receding tide of life.

Carmencita jumped to her feet. 'Pour more water! Pour more water!' she cried, and her little nostrils quivered.

'It's no use', said the boy-priest. 'He's finished.'

'No, he's not', Carmencita became very angry. 'I won't have it! Kick it! Go on! Kick it, I tell you.' The boy looked doubtfully at the massive, mutilated lump that heaved about from side to side as if it had heard the command in Carmencita's voice. He took a step forward, and as he did so, the eel lifted its head an inch or two off the earth for one final thud.

'Do it yourself', he retorted hastily, and stepped back.

Carmencita tossed her little head and tripped down the steps. 'I'll show you!' she said and marched forwards into the shambles.

'Come back!' shouted her nurse. 'Come back! It'll strangle you!' But Carmencita was strangely angry and took no notice. 'Look!' she cried and kicked at the remains of the eel with her little white kid shoes. 'Look!' she cried contemptuously. 'Why, it's dead already!'

And she kicked it again. 'What a shame! Why weren't you more careful with what you were doing?' she demanded of the two women. You killed it much too soon.' And she turned away in disgust at their clumsiness. Suddenly her excitement mounted again and she clapped her hands at her satellites.

'Let's get married all over again! Come along! Find my veil, somebody, and who has take my wreath away? Come on! Let's get married all over again, shall we? All over again!' And as she repeated this almost dreamily, she threw her arms round the neck of the boy groom with an energy that staggered him in his tracks, drew his face rapturously and crooningly between her little hands and kissed him voluptuously full on the mouth.

'Come and change your shoes at once', called Nannie.

'I shan't.'

'They're wet, I tell you. Come back at once, this very minute.' But Carmencita took no notice and went off with her troupe and a few minutes later her marriage lines were being cried aloud again to the four corners of San Salvador. But now Nannie was to be seen tagging faithfully behind, carrying a dry pair of shoes which Carmencita persistently refused to change into, with much stamping of feet and annoyance, till somebody suggested that it might be time for lunch and she suddenly sighed and announced that she felt very tired and held up her arms for Nannie to pick her up, who then gathered her to her faithful bosom, carrying her homeward, while Carmencita displayed the most innocent charm of sleepyheadedness imaginable. Ah, Carmencita!

Sunday was memorable; the fiesta of Saint Peter and Saint Paul. The Ermita chapel bell clapped merrily through the morning and the eleven o'clock service was crowded to the door. At least twenty people attended.

'Are you going to watch the Castillos y Torres on the beach this morning?' Juanet enquired. 'It is in honour of Casals' saints day, you know. The drum and pipe went by a few minutes ago, so they are probably getting ready to start.'

Castles and towers is an ancient festival practice in the old province of Tarragona, but this was the first occasion on which I had seen it. I made my way to the sands in front of Casals' gardens and soon learned that a group of young men had come down from Vendrell to honour their illustrious citizen in this way. Even as I took up my position the heaviest of the youths were preparing the base on which the others were to climb. Experimentally, they dug their feet into the sand and straightened their calves and thighs. The drum began to beat slowly, the pipe began its preliminary flourish before ascending the scale in sympathy with the second group of four athletes who prepared to ascend on the shoulders of the first quartet. They were all dressed in white shirts and trousers and wore red sashes about their loins and boinas on their heads. This second group hesitated and swayed, but eventually settled themselves fairly confidently. Then the third group, with quick agility, leaped upon their shoulders in turn, rocking the whole structure perilously. We all shouted apprehensively. But again the living castle steadied down into compactness. But then the next two assayed to clamber up these three stories. They were only slender boys; one stuck out his tongue unconsciously, with the strain of making his way upwards. There was a sudden sway from side to side, and down they all fell in a moment, collapsing on the sand while the music stopped and the bystanders laughed encouragingly. Then they tried again, and again they failed at the fourth storey.

At the third time the drum began to beat more insistently and the piper took longer breaths and produced prodigious flourishes. And now they got to the fourth storey and maintained their positions. Then the drum suddenly broke into double-beats and the piper held a high long drawn note. Up climbed the mascot child, like a cat, grinning, grinning as he clutched first at this man, then at another. Up he went, and at last there he stood at the topmost scaffolding of firm and proud-poised limbs. Out came a miniature banner which he waved about from side to side in the little morning breeze that blew off the sea. The pipe stopped – drum ceased – and they all gave forth their piercing, hooting cry of triumphant salute. 'Hui ! Hui! Hui! Huiiiii!' They down they fell, in miraculously true formation, and we cheered .and clapped. I thought it was all over. But no! They decided to do it once more, just to show that they could. And once more in honour of San Pablo and Casals the castle on the sands took shape. Then they went into the grounds of Casals' house to drink his health and we all drifted away home to lunch, or to picnic on the beach.

And now I was to experience the first occasion in my life on which I drank champagne. There was to be quite a gathering that evening at Casals' home and several of his friends had come down to spend the day together first and we had generally agreed to have a lunch party at the Ermita and to toast the maestro in style.

The wealthy patron of music in Barcelona and of Casals' orchestra in particular brought over half a dozen bottles in the car with his wife and numerous children, and as we sat he sent a bottle over to Casals' home with our compliments. Juanet and his wife had prepared a long table for us under the fig-tree's shade near the water-tank and the meal was a merry one. All went well till we reach dessert and the time of opening the champagne. There was plenty for everyone and our wine host insisted on replenishing our glasses all round. It is true we had already drunk red Sitges wine with the paella and chicken, but it was the cumulative effect of the second glass of champagne that produced an immediate and strange effect on the women. The singer, who had been eating her way steadily through the solid fare and had only contributed ejaculatory remarks to the conversation, suddenly burst into loud sobbing and without restraint heaved with woe for her absent husband. We patted her hands, then her back, but she went on crying. But when the wealthy business man said something cutting about this behaviour to his wife, she at once replied with a peevish sharpness that made him flush, and they turned their backs on the rest of the company and fell to quarrelling in an undertone. Next, the German girl all at once pushed back her chair and stood up. There was a puffed up look on her face that I had never seen before. Her eyes dwindled into slits, and there was an oddly piggish expression about her face as she pulled at the arm of the young conductor sitting next to her and dragged him away with her towards the garden path. He looked a little sheepish but acquiescent and away she led him through the hedge at the bottom of the kitchen garden and out of sight, while we tried not to look at one another. For though they were out of sight, they were not out of our range of sound, and we could distinctly hear the dry reeds bend and break as the couple sank down in the bed these offered.

'German pig', exclaimed the wealthy man's wife in disgust and we all lifted our eyebrows in polite Spanish fashion and tried not to hear what was going on beyond the hedge.

Then, strangely, I had a queer feeling that the present was being blurred before me and that I was experiencing events that had not yet existed. A moment ago, the woman opposite me – wife to one of the organisers of the business side of Casals' orchestra in Barcelona – had been laughing gently and playing with the baby in her lap. He was their only boy and the joy of his four little sisters as well as of the parents. Suddenly, in the midst of an opaque circle, as it seemed to be, I saw her dressed all in black, stricken with sorrow and gazing down at the child who was in some dreadful convulsion on her knee. I was too bewildered to cry out, though I found myself making what was meant to be a warning gesture. Her husband turned and stared at me curiously, but his wife continued to look as though she shared my tragic dream. Then the scene cleared again; I found myself rubbing my eyes and looking across the table, saw her dressed in her white flowered frock again as before. But as I looked, she gave me a sharp, involuntary sigh, as if she had wakened from a sleep in which she had been crying, and for a little while she sat silent, unsmiling, and the baby lay still upon her knee.

What could it mean? The children left the table and the rest of us sat rather thoughtfully for several moments.

'I always say champagne is a waste of money', said the man who had provided it. 'But nobody ever believes me when I say it is not weddings that make the women tearful, but the champagne. Now perhaps you will believe me. I'll keep it for funerals, in future.'

A year later, that companion of my waking dream was a widow. The tragedy shocked half of Barcelona. Her husband had been called out of the house one afternoon after lunch, a group of armed men had surrounded him, and he had been stood up against the wall and shot. The baby boy, now toddling, had followed his father to the door, and saw him fall bleeding at the mouth. The child ran in to his mother, and later that evening was stretched out lifeless in her lap after a series of convulsive fits. There was no political significance to the act of violence, the newspapers assured the public. He had more than once asked me to sing Purcell's setting of Dido's Lament, and I never had a more genuinely appreciative listener to my singing. 'Remember me, but ah! forget my fate!' 'What grand simplicity!' he would say, smiling slowly and shaking his head. 'Will you sing it again for us?'

The singer continued, with sighs and groans to demand our attention. She was cold, she was feverish, her head ached; she would not be able to sing that evening, she complained. The wealthy man's wife and I took her up to my room and put her down to rest on the bed. Then she became restless, tossing about on the counterpane and called on fate to have pity on her unhappiness. We were obliged to listen to her revelation of the tangled frustration of her emotional life, and I saw the other woman smile with faint irony when it became plain that her well-known affair with a noted poetical orator was of a strictly public nature, stimulating to the artistic vanity of both, but completely rhetorical in its romance. It was the bourgeois little husband she truly missed and moaned and panted for now and reticence was torn to shreds as she bewailed the long delayed return of his marital attentiveness. We gave her aspirin and left her to recover. 'Champagne', murmured my companion as we shut the door.

However, our singer was sufficiently restored to be in excellent voice for the evening at Casals' home, and I think she was a little surprised, therefore, when Casals turned and asked me to sing after she had only given us two or three items. She was even somewhat taken aback when he offered me his songs to sing in London. Simpleton that I was, I had never heard before that Casals wrote songs.

'I have some with English words', he said. 'By a poet whom the English greatly neglect.'

'Indeed? Who is that?' I asked, deeply interested.

'Matthew Arnold! He is my favourite poet.' I suppose I was unable to conceal my surprise for he went on: 'I see you don't agree with me!'

'No, no', I stammered, hastily trying to recall poems by Matthew Arnold. For the moment I could only think of The Forsaken Merman and I could scarcely imagine him setting that narrative to music. Now had it been Shelley, for instance ... Shelley was the bible I carried about with me in Spain at that time; it stayed under my pillow at night, it was my closest companion by day. It was the oracle by which I sought to guide my inexperienced way. In many, many of its pages bore the marks of tears. The margins and blank pages were scrawled with illegible and cryptic commentaries I had committed to writing in moments of excessively wrought sympathy with the poet's thought. But Arnold! I was not ill-read, but I had to confess my ignorance.

Casals was not ill-pleased. His point was proved.

'Come!' he said, 'I will play you one or two.' We moved towards the little piano. 'These verses are To Margaret.'

'Yes, yes. I remember now', I said. He nodded his head and began to play, picking out the vocal line from among the sweeping and swelling mass of arpeggio chords with which he had enriched the melody. I think he was satisfied with my attentiveness. I was the only English musician present and so only I could fairly judge the truth of his setting He played another; and another. As with the Mass, his interpretation was direct and sincere, but all the time I was wondering why this man with so fine an ear could have overlooked so many of our subtlest musicians of the English tongue and exalted Matthew Arnold above the rest.

But as he played I began to perceive that it was sincerity of thought he looked for and not the style and fashioning of sound. Was it the manliness with which Arnold faced the painful realisation that his vision of ideal life and the human consummation of rapture were not to be realised? Was it the calm but bitter acceptance that for most of us faith in an unseen other world flows in through one's being only when the sap and vitality of youth has ebbed away? Yes, I saw: it was all this, and something I was not yet old enough to know.

How long I continued to follow his musical train of feeling in this way I have now no idea, but at length he got up, rather abruptly, from the piano.

'NO!' he said, shaking his head and taking up his pipe, a German one, I noticed. 'No. The English neglect their finest artists.' He lit his tobacco and gave one or two contemplative puffs. 'Look at Tovey, for instance. I don't suppose you know any of his music, do you?'

'Well, as it happens, I do', I was glad to be able to say. He looked mildly surprised.

'Yes, of Tovey I *can* speak a little', I said. 'I have tried several times to sing his songs and to play some of his piano works, but really – really ...' I shook my head.

'Well?' Casals looked at me and waited for me to go on. Then I saw Eisenberg signalling to me from behind Casals' back. Suddenly I realised what that danger signal was trying to communicate. 'Is it a work of Tovey's you are rehearsing this summer?' I asked. 'They told me you are preparing a new English concerto, and I thought it might be something of Elgar's'.

'No. It is Tovey's. A fine work. A great work! He is your greatest composer, if you would but realise that fact.' I looked at him in astonishment. 'But nobody will acknowledge it, I cannot make anyone see what should be plain as daylight to you musical public. Well! I shall show them in Edinburgh next autumn!' he said, quietly, but with emphasis. He looked down at his hands as he spoke. Again once could see that the pads of his fingers were creased and depressed with excessive labouring. It was clear to us all that Casals was working against himself, against his own supreme skill. Yet somehow there was a moral conviction involved. Tovey worked by the laws of the great masters of tradition, therefore, he was one of them. There was stubbornness in Casals, as well as loyalty to the past. One could see that by looking at his mouth. The short upper lip expressed the same sweetness that his mother had looked down upon when he was a child, but there were folds of firmness about its corners which she would not have recognised.

'Well, I will take your advice and try to sing Tovey again', I said, thinking of my honest efforts in the past to breathe enthusiasm into those dreary Brahmsian-Scottish lieder.

Casals did not convince the British public that they had produced a composer of European vitality and stature, though he toiled mightily to champion his favourite and friend. Tovey was admired by many and loved by a few for the pawky punditry of his musical lectures. But that was all. Casals failed, his failure, however, was more glorious that the success of many others. His life, as we see it now, has proved to be one more manifestation of the spiritual greatness of Spanish individualism when it abnegates self for the gain of humanity.